AMAZING TESTIMONIES

TRISHA MANN-GRANT

You are an AMAZING TESTIMONY

To Jaem,
May God Bless you always. Thank you!

Reseda Church of Christ
11-17-18
Fall Concert
Reseda Mass Choir

Hugs

Trisha

208

Unless otherwise noted, Scripture quotations are taken from the New International Version (NIV)

ISBN 978-0-646-98377-6

TABLE OF CONTENTS

What matters most to God is the condition of one's Soul.

This Book Is Dedicated To

My grandmother, Ruth B. Randall

&

My mother, Carol E. Mann

*They both taught me
the true meaning of God's love,
how to share that love with others
and the power of prayer and faith.*

God answers and hears our prayers.

ACKNOWLEDGEMENTS

First and foremost, I thank God for loving me in spite of me. Thank you, Lord, for every idea and creative ability You have ever placed inside me, including this book. I am grateful for every trial You brought me through.

My husband, Tony Grant, for being my ROCK by encouraging and pushing me when I didn't think I could go on. Thank you, honey, for loving me and sharing your wisdom, heart, and life with me. I "Lovedore" you. *wink*

My children, Daniel and Dena, for motivating me every day to be a better mom and showing me the true meaning of unconditional love. Mama Bear loves you.

My mom, Carol, for being a praying mother and wearing holes in the carpet on her knees, talking to God on my behalf. Thank you also, Mom, for setting your dreams and desires aside to make sure Tasha and I never went without. I know I drove you crazy at times, but you loved me anyway. Hey, Mom, it's never too late for those dreams to come true.

My grandmother, Ruth, who is no longer with us, but her teachings, ethics, morals, values, prayers, and beautiful smile will remain inside my heart always.

My sister, Tasha, for all her prayers and the personal and legal advice she's given me for my career over the years, including *Amazing Testimonies*. Not to mention, she is one of the best big sisters anyone could have.

My cousin, Yusuf Ali El, has inspired me to write since I was a child. He is a phenomenal author, publisher and poet.

My business consultant, Hugh Mitchell Bouvier, for his sound advice, wisdom, and patience.

My "Bestie," Chris Williams, who helped sponsor me to get this book made. Not only did he co-design the cover with me, he illustrated the front and back cover and was patient through all my calls, texts and emails.

Reuben Wanjala, for being the vessel that helped bring *Amazing Testimonies* into fruition. It has truly been a journey Reuben. I pray blessings for you and your family.

My editor, Jessica Tilles, for coming on board at the eleventh hour per Vivica's request. Thank you for making this book a

priority with your busy schedule and for always being so pleasant to talk to.

Thank you Johnetta Kaleche Howard for your last minute touch of "catching" those things I missed. You are a blessing.

Everyone who contributed their life experiences in this book and took the time to share their *Amazing Testimonies* to encourage others.

To all of those who have prayed for me, thank you and God Bless you.

Love all, trust a few, do wrong to none.

- William Shakespeare

INTRODUCTION

How many times have I started writing and working on this book? Honestly, I've lost count. There were times I lost hope and for many years I just sat *Amazing Testimonies* on a shelf to collect dust.

Sometimes, I would even embarrass myself when someone would ask, "What are you working on these days, Trish?" The minute I mentioned this book, their response would slap me in my face. "Oh wow, you're still working on that?"

The interesting thing is that when I would set my mind on being very serious about getting it written, something would happen to distract or deter me from accomplishing my goal.

In June 2015, I had a minor stroke within a few weeks of restarting this book. I was fully recovered by November, but was determined to do phone interviews while I lay in bed, if necessary. I did just that.

The moment I started working hard on *Amazing Testimonies* again, a spirit of laziness, procrastination, and a lack of interest in getting it done came over me very strong. I prayed hard against that dark cloud that covered me, and God gave me the strength to pick up my computer and continue my writing quest.

Immediately and unexpectedly, I went through a short period of excruciating back spasms that hit me out of the blue; no back injuries or previous problems, just unexplained debilitating pain.

Once again, after recovering, I started working on the book. Then my son was injured at work. DISTRACTIONS! These are just a few events that took place during this same year, so imagine what the previous years have looked like and how I allowed the distractions or attacks to deter me. Even toward the end of the whole process of finishing this book, I was faced with unexpected and disappointing challenges that have taught me a huge lesson on how to deal with others for my future books. I am no longer deterred, but instead extremely DETERMINED, and I speak LIFE into *Amazing Testimonies* being a blessing.

3

THE BIRTH OF AN IDEA

In 2000, God gave me an idea to write a book called *Amazing Testimonies* that would be compiled of various true stories of how people have triumphed through the extreme challenges of life.

I remember thinking at that time, *A book, How in the world am I going to do that?* Days after receiving this divine revelation, I met a man who was passing out bread to the homeless from the back of his gym. He introduced himself to me as Pastor David. He told me he was a prophet of God and a weight trainer that ministered to his clients and spread God's Word on the streets to the homeless and the gangbanger. We talked briefly and Pastor David offered me some bread, then looked at me and said, "Sister, God told you to write a book. I see you writing this book at a desk. He wants you to be obedient."

CONFIRMATION

The Lord has a funny way sometimes of "nudging" you to do something and then placing someone in your path to confirm what He placed on your heart, but the rest is up to you.

God gave Moses the staff as an extension of the Divine power of The Holy Spirit. However, it wasn't until Moses stretched the staff over the water that the Red Sea parted. Every time Moses used the staff, he performed an action with it and had the faith behind it, knowing the extension of God's power would produce a mighty outcome through it. I was given an idea and God was kind and loving enough to give me unquestionable confirmation through one of His Prophets.

I remember an experience with being given a prophecy at the age of fifteen. The minister was so accurate on what God gave him to speak into my life, it was almost scary. Since then, I have had many experiences of people either walking up to me on the street and giving me a "word" or being at church and the pastor or church member speaking to me there.

All the true, God-given prophetic messages I have received have come to pass or are still in the making. I also realize there are quite a few "Prophe-liars" out there, so I ask God to lead me as well to discern whether a message for me is truly for me and from Him. In fact, I prefer to hear from Him myself, period. He speaks to anyone willing to have an ear to hear.

I, too, have been used from time to time as the messenger and people's response has been, "How did you know all of that?" I tell them that God was just using me at the time to be a vessel for Him to get His message across. I can never take credit for what God has done. He gets all the Glory. Most of the time, I don't even remember what I said, but I knew it was the power of The Holy Spirit working through me. In the same way I felt the confirmation of The Holy Spirit letting me know that Pastor David's words to me were true.

Then the question was, "What would I do next?"

OBEDIENT OR OBEDI-NOT?

Years ago, I was given a spiritual task to complete and I slowly, very slowly, took a stab here and there at this book. First, I called my sister, Tasha, who is a lawyer in New York, and she quickly drew up a Deal Memo for me to give anyone to sign that allowed me to publish or video their testimonies. I called a few friends and talked to a few of their friends and then I got sidetracked. This cycle of starting and stopping the *Amazing Testimonies* project has been consistent for too long.

Here I am, after beating myself up again, at the end of 2015, entering 2016, starting the cycle one more time. I am embarrassed, ashamed and filled with remorse when I think of all the lives I could have touched over all these years if I had just been obedient.

In the Word, Paul speaks of obedience being better than sacrifice.

I even wonder sometimes how I might not have struggled so much, had I just completed the task given to me. Would my life and career as an actress have been more fulfilling? I know I can't change the past, but I can influence the future. Yes, God has blessed me, my two children and now my husband over the years, but I often hear my mother say, "Only what you do for Christ will last." Furthermore, I know that life isn't about me; it's about me being used as a tool to touch others, inspire others, and hopefully bring them closer to God.

PURPOSE

Now that years have passed and technology has advanced, in addition to the book, *Amazing Testimonies*, I am inspired to not only do multiple volumes of the book, but to do the television show as well. I rebuke and block all distractions and attacks in the name of Jesus and I claim the Victory over the enemy's attacks against this plan for God's people. It is time to move forward and upward.

THE PLAN

I plan to speak to all nationalities about their life experiences and how they overcame their tests to reach their testimonies. Even though that negative place or situation is where they were, it's not who they are or where they are today. It's simple; a testimony can never be born without a TEST and sharing it with others can only BLESS.

Stop telling God how big your problems are and tell your problems how big your God is.

CHAPTER 1

STRANGER ANGELS

It is very difficult to believe something is true until you experience it for yourself. When I was a child, I heard about angels and at the age of twelve, my grandmother walked into the living room where I was lying on the couch very sick with the stomach flu. She came to a complete halt in awe of the sight before her eyes. She told me later that she saw a very tall male angel standing over me in a protective manner. I often thought of her story throughout the years and wished I could have seen for myself what she referred to as my Guardian Angel.

In my early thirties, I would start to see bright white orbs of light sporadically in various people's homes, including my own. When I told others who could relate, their response was, "Oh, you saw angels."

Just the other night, I was sitting at the foot of my bed, talking on the phone and for some reason I was staring down at the bottom part of my all black, unplugged, flat screen television. I was focused on the conversation I was having all while staring at my television intensely for no apparent reason. Suddenly, from my right to my left, three perfectly round, bright white orbs of light, the size of a grapefruit, rushed by the bottom of the TV, which was on the floor far from my bedroom window, which is on the second floor of my home, way above the street and car lights.

The orbs disappeared as they quickly passed the TV, as if they were chasing each other in a perfectly parallel formation. I was not afraid, but shocked. That was the last thing I expected to see and there was no explanation for the three balls of light, but I wasn't scared. Fear is generally associated with an evil presence or atmosphere and if your faith is weak, it can overcome you. After doing some research on the orbs, I realized some people have different views about their meaning, but many have experienced seeing them.

7

There are quite a few videos on YouTube that show you what the orbs I am describing look like. For example, on one video, there is a woman who was dying in a hospital room and her daughter captured on video the many angelic orbs of different shapes and sizes floating around the woman and her bed. Another video shows a congregation in praise and worship where countless large bright white orbs are floating over the congregation as they sing and pray. I believe they are angelic, but until I can back that up with some scripture, let's just say that is my opinion.

One early morning, when my children were very small, I woke up around three a.m. and saw someone moving in my room, but I wasn't fearful. One thing I've come to know about Godly encounters is that when a spiritual experience occurs, there is an atmosphere of peace. I turned my head toward the figure, which appeared to be a man wearing the most beautiful pearl white robe with a very detailed gold embroidered trim at the bottom of it and the same trim on the edges of the low hanging arms of the robe. What was interesting was that I couldn't make out a face, but what I quickly assessed to be an angelic being was also wearing a small white hat that resembled a Yarmulke worn by Jewish males with the same embroidery.

I impulsively wanted to jump up and greet my angelic visitor, but something inside me stilled me as I watched him move fluidly into my children's room. I say, "him" because I knew instinctively that the being was a male. I knew in my heart and spirit that he was there for protection and it seemed also for prayer. There was a strong sense of peace in the room and I was grateful to be able to witness it.

Throughout the years, I have heard people tell stories of angels coming to their aid in the form of a regular person. The moment each person would attempt to say, "Thank you," the angel would mysteriously disappear. The story of my mother's lifelong friend, whom I affectionately call Aunt Pat, who had Multiple Sclerosis, inspired me to interview her the next time I saw her. She told me, and hundreds of other people, this story.

The first time I sat down with my phone to do a voice recording with Aunt Pat, the phone wouldn't work so I tried another phone interview when I went back to visit her another time. Unfortunately, only a portion of the story recorded. I had a strong and urgent sense to go back to Aunt Pat's house in Pasadena and this time, videotape her testimony. She had been confined to a wheelchair and for many years at the mercy of others for help, but she was always laughing and smiling with an unspeakable joy. My mother happened to be visiting me in Los Angeles and I told her I wanted to see Aunt Pat and while there, try to get her testimony successfully this time.

My mom had already planned to visit her friend, so we made a special trip to Pasadena. As I climbed the stairs to her house to be greeted by that big beautiful, joyful smile of hers, I had a strong feeling that would be the last time I would climb those stairs to see this phenomenal woman who loved the Lord even more during her sickness than she did during her wild and free days. She was more than willing and surprisingly grateful to engage me, yet again, with her angelic experience. This time, there were no glitches.

The next time I saw Aunt Pat, shortly after that day, was in the hospital on her deathbed. I held her cold hand as she lay there with her eyes closed tight, while my husband, Tony, and I prayed over her. Then I leaned down and whispered in her ear, "See you one day soon, Auntie, I love you." Within moments, her eyes opened so wide. She looked right past me with her gaze fixed on something neither my husband, my daughter nor I could see.

She stared so intensely into the air; I knew she was seeing in the spiritual realm because I hadn't seen her eyes that big in years. Just as quickly as she had opened them, they were closed. I signed out of the hospital at 5:55 p.m. and within thirty minutes, I received a text from her daughter saying, "Mom is gone, but she waited for you to come."

I have the honor of sharing her story with you because each time Aunt Pat told it, she smiled with joy and even though I captured her on video this time, there were other details I remember her mentioning in past conversations about her experience that she didn't mention in the video, so I will do my best to recall those details that came from a truly amazing woman who never complained, even though she had every reason to. Instead, she was an example of having joy in spite of her health, losing both parents back-to-back, as well as many other situations she faced. Thank you, Aunt Pat, for being a wonderful example and for sharing your testimony with us all, I pray I do it justice.

AMAZING TESTIMONY
by:
TRISHA MANN-GRANT,
in remembrance of "Aunt Pat" who suffered from Multiple Sclerosis

IN THE NICK OF TIME

On my last visit to Aunt Pat's home, she told me and my mom that she was coming from the doctor's office in her mobile wheelchair one day and she decided to take a shortcut so she didn't have to go through all the traffic on the street. Unfortunately, this meant that she had to go across a railroad track that took her on the path toward her home. She said she had no idea that her tires were so thin that they would slip down between the track and the opening that was there. Her mobile wheelchair, which was extremely heavy, was now stuck in the train track and Aunt Pat was in a position that she recalled she couldn't get herself out of.

She said her chair wouldn't go back over the hump and she couldn't stand up and pull it over the hump because she was unable to walk. Aunt Pat knew that the train was going to come shortly around the corner where there was a curve, so she said this prayer aloud, "Lord, please have mercy on me. I'm not ready to go yet. I've got a lot of things I would like to do and if You would be graceful and merciful and deliver me from this, I'll be forever grateful."

I love my elders so much not only for their spiritual wisdom and strength but the old school phrases they use on us 'youngstas'. For example, I remember as I sat on the edge of my seat listening to her story and what happened next…this story never got old to me, Aunt Pat threw one of those old school terms at me and she said, "Low and behold, this man—I knew he had long hair and I knew he was a white man. He just walked over to the chair, without saying anything to me, and lifted me out of the hole." By the time she got across the track, after he lifted the wheel up, the train came.

She turned around to say "Thank you" right after he pulled her free from the track, but she said that he just disappeared. In previous conversations, she went into detail about a car wash not being far from the railroad track, but it was so busy and noisy that no one would have heard her even if she did scream for help. She fondly remembered her hero who she described as *wearing all white, average height, medium build and couldn't have been over one hundred fifty pounds.* She knew that he couldn't have gone away from her that quickly because it was a wide-open space and she definitely would have seen him still walking away but he vanished into thin air. Aunt Pat said she didn't see him go one way or the other, but she knew without a doubt that he was an angel of God sent here to save her.

I thanked Aunt Pat for taking the time once again to share her angelic experience, she just looked at me and said that she could tell that story anytime, anywhere and be thankful. Then she thanked me for the opportunity, and smiled, saying that she has told it a hundred times, but she always felt good about telling it.

Aunt Pat was special to me and she had an incredible sense of humor. I believe in my heart that the man, who saved her that day was indeed an angel. I wondered a few times how in the world could he have lifted her and the mobile wheelchair, which combined might have been about three hundred fifty pounds, with such ease without supernatural strength? All I can say is, "But God."

He sits high and He looks low.

AMAZING TESTIMONY
by:
IMANI DUDLEY-WALKER
Dancer for Aretha Franklin and other celebrities
Facebook: Imani Nakia

DOUBLY DUDLEY BLESSED

My second year of college, I moved off campus into a two-bedroom apartment and my roommate, who was my 'bestie' in high school, changed her mind about moving in with me, without any warning.

Unfortunately, I had already signed a one-year lease in my name. I was only expecting to pay my half of the rent, which was $430 a month. To this day, I don't know why she bailed out on me, but it put me in a bad position and I was forced to pay all the rent that was $860.00 a month.

I thank God for my refund check because it helped me pay the rent in advance for at least four months. Sometimes, my mom would help me out. However, there were a few times I was two or three weeks late with the rent and I was taken to court over it. From time to time, I would be blessed with dancing gigs, but it was always tight.

I searched diligently for another roommate and when I finally got one, she found a place that was just ten or twenty dollars cheaper than our current rent, and she moved out after only one month. Once again, I was left footing the entire bill.

I was eighteen and it was my first time having my own place, but it taught me how to be independent and be by myself. I prayed often, and there were times I didn't know how I would pay next month's rent. I was a full-time student, working gigs here and there. However, I was determined not to fail my second year.

One day, my sister, her best friend, and I wanted to celebrate her birthday. I was excited because I hadn't been to a nice restaurant in such a long time. So, we stepped out on a

12

wing and a prayer with very little money (between the three of us) in our pockets to share my sister's special day.

I remember sitting in the window at the restaurant and I looked up and noticed a man sitting in a Mustang looking at us. He waved and smiled, we all waved and smiled back, and then he drove off.

Five minutes later, our server walked up, handed us $100 and said, "The guy who was outside wanted me to give you guys this."

Now, the man never came to the table. In fact, I never saw him come into the restaurant and from where I was sitting; I could see everyone who walked through that door. He had just blessed us so we could pay for our meal. That was right on time because shockingly, we had run our bill up to $80, which was over the amount we had in our pockets and this meant we would've had to clean the dishes (laughs). It was as if he somehow knew what we were going through.

That was the strangest, yet most beautiful experience and we all knew that God was looking out for us completely. I believe in my heart that the man in the Mustang was an angel sent at the right time to bless us. I also managed to survive my one-year lease without an eviction and somehow God made sure that the rent was paid every month that year.

Never be afraid to trust an unknown future to a known God.

Corrie Ten Boom

AMAZING TESTIMONY
by:
PASTOR ARLAN SANCHEZ
Pastor of The Covenant Church in Pasadena, California
arlansanchez.com
thecovenantchurch.org

STRANDED

I've had many Spiritual visitations, but one in particular does stand out when I was a Bible College student. I was driving alone in the hills and my car was running thin on gas. I lived in a very hilly area, which sloped, and I was driving on fumes. I had an encounter where I was having a rough week and I knew in my heart that God was dealing with me in many different regards. I was struggling. It was a still night, the stars were out, the moon was on the horizon, and it was filling the atmosphere.

I knew the Lord was with me through school, but it was tough financially so I thought about quitting school. I was now starting to feel almost like I was experiencing abandonment and stillness. It was as if the Lord's presence wasn't there anymore. I felt like people wouldn't blame me if I gave up and I felt like I had the permission to be frustrated and give up. I read something recently that said just because you're anointed doesn't mean you're approved. King Saul had that with his prophecy, but he wasn't allowed to do it anymore.

And, here I was, driving alone in the hills. My car slowed down and finally just sputtered out of gas and came to a complete stop. I was too far away to walk back to campus, so I put my car in neutral, got out and started to push my own vehicle. There was no way I could communicate with anyone, even if there were cell phones back then, because I didn't have one. I was crying out to God, "Lord, I don't have the strength to make this happen and I can't push this car on my own! I can't leave this car here."

14

I was literally going uphill on an incline and I remember the street to this day. It was called Don Julian. I got behind the car and it was so heavy that my feet started to slip, so I went around the side of the car. I reached inside the car and pulled up the handbrake. I remember thinking, *Oh man, what is going on here? I need the strength to push this thing back home.* I prayed out to God again because people were driving down this road and they wouldn't stop to help me.

This place was really country and at least a mile and a half away from campus. There was nothing but hills, no homes or people hanging out. I was next to the big giant radio towers and no telling what was near that tower—jackrabbits, snakes, you just didn't know. I came back around the back of the car and started to push.

Out of nowhere, this guy came out and said in a very low, deep voice, "I got it man, get in and I'll push."

I said, "You'll push? How are you going to do that?"

I was a big man, but he repeated himself more emphatically with the same low, deep voice so I got into the car. I never saw his face because he had it down, but I saw his hands and they were big and massive. He pushed me up to the incline and into the street, and I started to coast. The car coasted left into the parking lot and I pulled over to say, "Thank you" but when I looked for him, he wasn't there. He was nowhere to be found.

There was nowhere for him to go. I instantly remembered God's word, *I give my angels charge over you to keep thee in all thy ways,* and I knew in my spirit that I had an angelic encounter. After realizing that my angelic help wasn't sticking around for gratitude, I continued to coast in my car all the way down until I reached the campus.

The next day, a buddy of mine put a couple of dollars in my pocket for gas. After sharing with him what had transpired, he reminded me that angelic visitations bring greater harvest and confirmation. They propel you and increase your faith and that encounter did just that.

Sometimes we are looking for a supernatural encounter in the heavens when God is looking to do the miraculous in our everyday lives. So, the next time your natural resources have depleted, be reminded that God has angelic agents ready to invade your natural atmosphere.

AMAZING TESTIMONY
by:
JUDE PAGO and TRACYE PAGO
Filmmakers/Producers of the film, "RELATIONSHIPS"
Facebook: Jude Pago

HEAVEN MADE

Jude:

Tracye and I met in Smyrna, Georgia. We were having a hard time because I proposed to her and her mom opposed our decision. Her mother said she didn't believe God wanted us to get married.

Tracye was a college graduate and we had just met so her mom assumed I was trying to control her. We weren't sleeping around or doing anything crazy, but her mom was a single mother, protective of Tracye and she didn't trust me.

What she didn't know was that Tracye and I fasted and prayed about whether we should get married. We fasted for seven days straight, twice. Tracye had never fasted before in her life. We felt spiritually that God's answer was "Yes" after the first fast so we did it again for another seven days just to be sure. When I felt weak and wanted to break the fast, Tracye encouraged me to be strong and keep going. The funny thing was that I was the one who was always praying, going to church, and fasting before we met.

Tracye's mother wanted her to marry someone who was more established with money. I was living with a friend at the time and I didn't have a car or a house, but I was clean, didn't smoke or drink and we met in church. Every time her mother would say what I didn't have materially, God would bless me with it in a very short amount of time. It was still very discouraging to have her mother's disapproval.

One day after church, Tracye and I decided to go for a walk and talk. We were at a park and it was designed strange. The park was situated on the side of a hill and you had to walk across the street to disappear out of sight. There was a sidewalk

16

and a parking lot, so to leave the park would take a while. A very friendly white guy sat next to us on the park bench and we started talking. He had these amazing blue eyes. He said, "Hi, how ya doing?" We told him we were newly engaged and then we just opened up about our situation and he had an answer for everything. There was a presence about him, he seemed to know everything that was going on with us, and he had so much wisdom and insight.

That was a pivotal point because I was considering not getting married because of her mom. I appreciated the talk and he inspired me to go ahead and marry her. We got up from the park bench where he was still sitting, we took only a few short steps, and we both said, at the same time, "Was that an Angel? Nah." We both turned back to look at him, but he had disappeared. Again, the way the park was made; it would have taken him forever to get out of plain sight. We both thought that had to be an angel and there was no way he could have known the things he knew. There was no way he could have left without us seeing him.

A couple of months later, Tracye and I got married. We waited until our wedding night to have sexual intercourse and it is not often when a couple comes together sexually, that they climax at the same time. The presence of God came over us while we made love and we both began to weep simultaneously. We both heard God say, "I love you and thank you for waiting." By consulting God about getting married, we believe He took it seriously. God became a part of our dating process and marriage and God has been faithful to us.

Tracye:

I remember one time I was yelling at God during a difficult time and I said, "You said You would be there!" I was praying and so afraid before our marriage, but God showed up. I had never really talked to God before my fast. God let me know to trust Him in the relationship and He would be there. After we got married and would have some challenges, I would tell God, "You said You would make a difference," and He would work it out every single time.

What I remember about that angel that was so amazing was that he was a stranger who seemed to really care. We gained so much strength from talking to him. He was so encouraging. I remember thinking, How does this stranger know and care so much about two young people? In Georgia, it was not normal

for a white person to engage so friendly with black people. He was definitely older than we were, but he had a youthful glow.

Jude:

He was positive about everything, but I will never forget about a guy I once encountered. My car broke down in Thousand Oaks and I worked in Hollywood so it took me three hours to get to work and home. While I was on the train, I saw a black dude about six-two and I will never forget him lying on the floor on the metro with his bike on the wall. He was enjoying himself. I was thinking, This guy is confident, just having a good time, not caring what others think. I wish I could be that free.

I had been studying about demons and angels at that time, so I was walking off the train and up the stairs and suddenly, he was walking right next to me with his bike on his shoulders and I thought, *Wow, he got off that train fast and I never saw him get up, okay.* I had a book out called, *He Came to Set the Captives Free* and I was reading it and walking. This same guy walked by me and said, "I like that one." I'm thinking, *Wow, that's never happened to me, especially with this book here.* I got on the bus, I looked up, and the guy with the bike was also on the bus. There was something special about him, I had been intensely in God's presence, and I could see everything spiritually about everyone.

When I sat down, a young man immediately sat next to me and I sensed he was a demon. I was prepared for him to attack me because I could tell he was under the influence of drugs and he was tweaking. I felt the presence of evil strongly. I don't remember him getting up and I don't remember my friend with the bike getting off the bus, but all I knew was that one minute I was reading the book and somehow it disappeared. The last thing I remember was a lady with a suitcase who got on the bus. She had a very dark presence about her as well and as I watched her, she began to twitch and snarl.

It was the strangest thing and I was so upset about my book vanishing. My daddy sold books so I valued them. After that, God brought me revelation about heaven and hell. I often think about the man with the bike. It was something about him that was different from everyone—his calm voice, his free and happy spirit and just with those few words he spoke to me there was a connection. I can still see his face and even though nothing spectacular happened, I feel like he was an angel in disguise. I named him Raphael.

18

AMAZING TESTIMONY
by:
TOI NOLEN SMITH KING TOI
Author
Twitter: @therealtoi88

THE DREAM

My first angelic experience and invitation I remember was the acknowledgement of my journey. I was blessed to see my one hundred three-year-old great-great-grandmother. She turned ill and was in the hospital and we had to hurry and get there. She was short like me and thinner, and while in the hospital, she had blown up five times her size. She had some form of cancer that I didn't understand much about. I remember holding her hand and having a conversation with her.

That night, I went back to her house and I was very sad and asking God questions like, "Why and what is happening?" Everyone went to bed and it was late. I was lying there and this cat was sitting on the nightstand next to me. I thought that was a little weird and she started meowing and meowing. I reached out to pet her and tell her that it's going to be okay, she's going to a better place. The phone rang after that and everyone said, "She's gone."

Later, after the funeral, I felt a presence in the basement. The second I turned on the little lamp on the nightstand, in the corner was my great grandmother sitting and rocking in the rocking chair. I was scared and at one point, she stopped rocking, took her foot, leaned forward, and said, "You are an anchor." And then she was gone. I've never seen her to this day.

My grandfather and step-grandfather were also both intricate forces in my life. I lived with my step-granddad and granddad lived in Maywood. I have tons of fond memories of both of them that I strongly remember. No one told me these stories. In my thirties, I was living at Graymoor in Olympia

Fields, Illinois. A lot of actors, football players, doctors, and affluent people lived in this Jewish community. One day, I went to breakfast with a friend and two brothers. When we got back home, we pulled in the driveway and my mom called me about an accident involving my brothers.

Three weeks before the call, I had a dream that I was with my mom, grandma and brother's friend and we were at a sporting event. My grandmother had a green Tahoe. In the dream, both my grandfathers had gotten into a bad accident while driving a green Tahoe and the Tahoe flipped over. My grandmother told me to get down there because I was the only one that could get out of the stands and get to the track where they were. They loved horses and racing, but it was like they were the horses.

When my brothers had the accident, my brother had the same truck as my grandmother. The dream instantly came back and I thought I was going to have a heart attack! It felt like a movie and suddenly everything around me moved in slow motion. I remember this lady at the site of the accident praying the blood of Jesus over them. We got to the hospital and they were fine with minor injuries. Three weeks after that dream, my biological grandfather died in his sleep. I thought to myself, Lord, what does this mean?' We buried him on my ex-husband, Tony's birthday, at the time we were still together. For a while, I was devastated. Three weeks later, my step-grandfather took a turn for the worse with Amyloidosis Cancer. Nothing could be done, no treatments or anything. He was ready to die.

One night, my mom and grandmother called me down to the hospital and told me they needed to speak with me. I had been talking and laughing with Daddy at his bedside and I whispered in his ear, "I know you gotta go, but please come back and check on me, TJ and Tam. I don't want you to go, but I know." I was crying profusely when Mom and Grandma said, "Stop it, you are the strength of this family, you are the backbone!" I didn't understand that because they were the elders and I thought they should be praying. They said, "You're holding him here and you have to let him go."

He asked me to get him some Taco Bell and that night as I brushed his teeth and helped him rinse out his mouth, he said, "I'm tired and I want you to know you're my baby and you'll always be my baby." That next morning, I was called back to the hospital. He was walking around delirious and the staff informed me he hadn't expired yet, so they sent him home. I was there when he got home. I said, "I told you, Daddy, you weren't leaving me." He smiled. I was happy.

I went home and the kids and I built a bonfire and made hot dogs. A short while later, my grandma called and said, "Get back here." The minute I walked in the room, he gasped for air. I loved him so much. That man gave me life. He never hurt me. He was so good to me. Both my grandfathers were the only men in my life that never hurt me. They never told me no, they never said, "No you can't be a queen." They told me I could be whatever I want to be. When they chastised me, it hurt my feelings more than anything. He died.

When I moved to Mississippi three months ago, I went to Walmart around 11:00 a.m. I was looking up in the sky and it looked like it was going to storm, but the sky was so beautiful. I was feeling down about transitioning to a new state and my arthritis was acting up. I pulled into the parking lot, looking up at the sky and having a moment, talking to my grandfather, telling him, "Daddy, I miss you." I prayed to God, "Lord, I just need something right now."

This truck pulled up next to me. I finally got out of the car. The truck was glowing like a halo was over the door. It was not a glare it was definitely a glow on the side of it. I looked down and saw the sign on the door, which read Ratliff Construction. My grandfather's last name was Ratliff and he was born and raised in Mississippi. The angel of the Lord spoke to me at that moment and said, "Lo, I am with thee always until the end of time." A sense of joy came over me and the sadness left me.

I came home and researched in the Bible what the angel said to me and it was in Matthew 28:21, which reads, *Lo, I am with you always even until the end of the world.* I texted my grandmother, told her what happened and sent her a picture of the truck. She texted me back: *He's with you everywhere you go.* My grandfather still comes and visits me often. He kept his promise to watch over me and over the kids.

My step-grandmother died from a broken heart six months to the date after he died.

AMAZING TESTIMONY
by:
HUSSEIN MANN
Father of Author Trisha Mann-Grant
Humanitarian
Instagram: @husseinmann

THE VISITATION

Approximately 1950 in Chicago, Illinois, I may have been about seven years old and I was attending a Catholic grammar school. On this notable day, the nuns showed our class a movie on a large white screen using a reel tape projector. The short story was filmed in a South American country.

In the story, a friend of a slightly intoxicated alcoholic brought the alcoholic to a catholic priest for counsel. The priest asked the alcoholic what he thought would happen to him if he died. The alcoholic replied, "Don't worry, Father, when I die I will say, 'God forgive me' and I will be forgiven of all my sins."

A few days later, a car hit the alcoholic, with his friend by his side on his knees trying to revive him. The priest ran to his aid, but the friend stood up and said, "It's too late, he's gone."

The priest asked, "Did he say 'God forgive me' as his last words?"

His friend replied, "No, Father, he said, 'You crazy driver, why don't you watch where you're going?' And then he died."

Little did I know that watching this movie would one day save my life, even though I never became an alcoholic. Years later, after I was grown and married, I lay in bed asleep next to my pregnant wife. I saw a bright white light coming toward me. It was small at first, but it grew larger as it came closer to me. As the light reached a halfway point, I began to hear the voices of a thousand angels singing God's praises and each one had a different song to sing. As the light came closer and closer, their voices became louder and louder.

I wanted to join them, but I didn't feel worthy. I wanted to make sure I went to heaven with them, but in a split second, I

22

remembered the story of the priest and the alcoholic from my childhood. I said, "God forgive me." The light came closer and again I said, "God forgive me." Now I was fully engulfed by the light. I could feel intense love and the angels' voices had reached their glorious full volume. Once more I cried out, "God forgive me!" Then the light broke away from me. I knew that this was God.

The light moved away slowly at the same rate of speed in which it approached me. The angels' voices also receded. Then there was the void of blackness. No dreams, no sound, just me alone in a black void of nothingness. I was there for only a short period of time, but I knew it was not a place I wanted to stay in.

Next, I felt my body being shaken by my father-in-law. He said, "Hussein, wake up! The gas was left on in the stove and the whole house is filled with gas!" He continued to shake me and I slowly opened my eyes. I looked over at my wife and saw her mother shaking her and yelling at her to wake up. I looked on the other side of my mother-in-law and I saw that they had opened the window.

The curtains were flowing from the strong wind blowing through the wide-open window. The curtains were waving like the American flag, declaring victory over death.

His eye is on the Sparrow and I know He watches over me.

SCRIPTURES ABOUT ANGELS

²Do not forget to show hospitality to strangers, for by so doing some people have shown hospitality to angels without knowing it.
Hebrews 13:2

¹⁰For it is written, He will command his angels concerning you to guard you carefully.
Luke 4:10

²⁰See, I am sending an angel ahead of you to guard you along the way and to bring you to the place I have prepared.
Exodus 23:20

²⁶In the sixth month of Elizabeth's pregnancy, God sent the angel Gabriel to Nazareth, a town in Galilee, ²⁷to a virgin pledged to be married to a man named Joseph, a descendant of David. The virgin's name was Mary. ²⁸The angel went to her and said, "Greetings, you who are highly favored! The Lord is with you." ²⁹Mary was greatly troubled at his words and wondered what kind of greeting this might be. ³⁰But the angel said to her, "Do not be afraid, Mary; you have found favor with God. ³¹You will conceive and give birth to a son, and you are to call him Jesus. ³²He will be great and will be called the Son of the Most High. The Lord God will give him the throne of his father David, ³³and he will reign over Jacob's descendants forever; his kingdom will never end."
Luke 1:26-31

¹⁰In the same way, I tell you, there is rejoicing in the presence of the angels of God over one sinner who repents.
Luke 15:10

Our Guardian Angels are closer to us than anything except the love of God.
- Eileen Elias Freeman

CHAPTER 2

SUPERNATURAL HEALING
AND FAITH

In June 2015, weeks after I decided to start working on *Amazing Testimonies* again with the determination to finish it, I had a stroke at the age of forty-five. I have always had the habit of pushing my stress deep down inside of me as if it just didn't exist and sometimes I was oblivious to the fact that I was stressed. I'm not alone in this misguided behavior and I personally know others who do the same thing. I've witnessed for myself that eventually the stress we ignore finds a way to come out and will either affect our skin, our hair, blood pressure, our neurological system, bring headaches, anxiety, depression or more. Now if you couple poor eating habits with lack of proper sleep and stress, you are asking to be a stroke victim.

I was ripping and running during the whole month of May into June and not sleeping well. This normally happened when my husband was out of town filming his television show or touring with Stage-plays for long periods of time; I just couldn't sleep through the night. I guess I feel safer when he's home and happy to know that I'm not alone because other women I've talked to experience the same thing. During the height of my "unknown stress," it was my daughter's eighth grade graduation and not only was I planning her celebration for the family, but I was preparing for my mother to come to town.

I had just gone through a tumultuous time about nine months prior to the graduation with my son who, thank God has come a long way and is much better. I will save his testimony for a future book. Even though it had been nine months since all that stress, he still wasn't completely out of the woods during this time and I was still concerned about him. Everything was on me to plan this graduation celebration and I felt completely overwhelmed, but I kept going like a car that is almost out of gas and hasn't had an oil change in ages.

We successfully made it through the graduation and celebration and a few days later, I was out with my mom, daughter, husband's good friend, Vince, and his wife, Imani; we had gone to a restaurant after church to do one of my favorite things—eat. Thank God, I have a high metabolism. I ordered grilled salmon; we face-timed my husband, Tony, joked around with him and then within moments after ending the phone call, I had lost my desire to eat another bite. I suddenly felt nauseous and closed in. Everyone at the table knew how much I love food so they immediately knew something was wrong when I pushed my plate aside.

I got up to go outside because I was feeling dizzy and claustrophobic and I needed some space. Vince told me later that a doctor who was having lunch there also noticed me and approached him to see if I was okay. He said, "She doesn't look good. You guys might want to get her to the hospital." Unbeknownst to me, Vince called Tony right back and said, "I think something's wrong with Trish and she was just talking about going to the radio station to do her show." I had a lovely guest, Jennifer Hobson, whom I personally invited, flying in from Texas to be on Gospel Rhythms with me and GR creator, Roceania Williams; for our weekly live and globally U-streamed radio show. I could not flake on her so I had to get myself together. It was hot outside, so even though I went to get some space, I still wasn't able to catch my breath the way I wanted to. I finally came back in and everyone was concerned about me.

As we were all walking to the car, my phone rang and it was Tony. "Honey, you okay?" he asked. I knew instantly that he had spoken to Vince and I turned back to give Vince a, "Really Brother?" look. "I just had a little spell, but I feel much better." I responded. "I want you to go home and rest, okay?" he gently commanded. "But honey, my guest today flew in to be on the show, I must be there and then I'll come home and rest, promise." "Trisha Mann-Grant," he said, this time with a tone. "Go home and lay down because obviously, something is wrong. Now if you love me like you say you do, you will not stress me out by making me worry about you." Yes, he went there and I heard myself say, "Okay." My heart was saying something else but I had the audacity to be upset with him and

upset with Vince for telling him. Sometimes people just simply care and we need to let them.

On the way home, I didn't know how I was going to break the news to Jennifer, who had just spent money on a plane ticket to come all the way to Los Angeles just so I could say, "Sorry, I won't be there to interview you." My mom and I went in the house and I sat down for a short while, I felt better and my daughter asked me could she go over a friend's house. At that moment, I decided to go against the wishes of my hubby and make my way to the radio station. I guess Dena heard me tell my mother what my plans were and I took her to her friend's house not knowing that Tony would call her to tell her to let me rest and not bother me for the rest of the day.

"Mom just dropped me off at my friend's house and she went to do the radio show." That would be an issue I had to deal with for a long time after. Obedience is better than sacrifice, and yes, when you have a good, godly, loving man who has your best interest at heart, listening to him is not a bad thing to do at all. I drove slowly to the station, which is about forty-five minutes away, depending on the famous, 405 highway traffic. I felt terrible.

I had convinced myself that I did come home and get "a little" rest and I was up for the cause. I prayed to God for supernatural strength, made it to the station, greeted Jennifer and the show was good. I got through the show with no problems, gave my guest some love and I drove home. The sick feeling started to come back as I was driving on the 405 and I couldn't wait to get home and in the bed, but then the call came from my husband. I will spare you the details of that call, but I had disappointed him greatly, which made me feel even worse.

The next day I took my mother to the airport and afterwards I went to the doctor's office for a full checkup, blood tests, and EKG. Imani, whom I refer to as my lil' sis, went with me and because I forgot to bring my insurance card, I told the doctor I would go home after my visit with him and bring back the card. By now, I was hungry, so Imani and I went to a restaurant next door to his office and got something to eat. This time, right after I ate, I felt ten times worse than I did the other day when I felt sick. My mobility was failing and it seemed like all my energy had left my body. I was more nauseous than the first time it happened, so we sat in the car for a moment and Imani offered to drive me home.

When we arrived at my house, I was beginning to feel better so I decided to grab the insurance card and go back to the doctor's office with every intention of telling him what just happened to me after eating. When I reached my front door, I heard a loud crunch sound behind me and I dreaded to turn around because I knew it was my car. A male driver had knocked my driver's side mirror clean off the door of my Mercedes Benz that I had just upgraded to a year before.

That was a scene for a slow-motion moment. I am sure the look on my face was priceless especially at the sight of watching the man continuously drive down the street as if he had not done anything. I ran into the street chasing his car screaming, "Hey! Stop! You hit my car! Stop!" The man stopped midway down the street and just sat there. My son came up at the same time and saw me chasing this man and he ran up to the car going off on the driver using some colorful language that I know I didn't teach him. I stopped my son in his tracks, "Hey! That is not how we talk to people so bring it down and let's find out what happened." I'm thinking maybe the man had a heart attack or passed out or something.

My son promptly apologized and brought his voice down a notch, but by now the man in the car was terrified, in fact, too terrified to drive at all. My son parked his car for him and the man walked back with me to my car while I wrote down his license and insurance information; then I called my insurance company. The guy told me, in a very thick Indian accent, that he had just started driving for the first time and I happened to be his first accident victim. *Gee, what an honor,* I thought. "I hope I'm your last accident victim too." I told him.

After all that business, Imani and I rushed back to the doctor's office and I went in with the insurance card and told his secretary how sick I'd gotten at the restaurant. When I got back in the car to take off, I looked up and my doctor and his secretary were running toward the car. I looked at Lil' sis and said, "This can't be good." My doctor said, "I want you to go to the emergency room right now." Those were words that I really did not want to hear. I said, "Doc, I feel better and I'm leaving town in a few days so I have to get this car in the shop because my mirror just got knocked off." He looked at me like I had two heads and calmly, yet emphatically said, "I think you need to worry about your car later and go to the emergency room now."

I heard my husband's voice of reason in my head and I knew this was not the time to be hardheaded, so Imani drove me to the emergency room. Once the nurse took my blood pressure and saw that it was 175 over 80 which was high, they took me straight to the back, did an EKG, and gave me a bed so they could do multiple tests. Hours later, after some of the results had come back, a very small- framed Asian doctor came to talk to me. "It looks like you've had a mild stroke Mrs. Grant. We are going to do an MRI before I confirm that, but that's my guess." He ended up sending me home with the possibility of having a TIA (Transient Ischaemic Attack), which is a mini-stroke. The next day my speech was badly slurred and I was walking funny.

My friend Margo, whom a few years earlier had a supernatural miraculous healing, came to follow me to drop the car off before I went out of town. When she arrived and I went outside to talk to her, she said, "Trisha, are you okay? You are slurring your words." I told her I was fine and the doctor told me to get some rest. When I walked away, she was watching me walk sideways. "Un unh, I'm calling my husband so he can follow us while I drive your car to the shop and we are taking you to the hospital." I didn't have the energy to argue and I was starting to be a little concerned, too.

Daryl got there and the minute he saw me he placed his hand on my head and said the most beautiful prayer for me. Margo drove my car and Daryl followed us to the dealership. By the time we got there, I was slumped down in the seat and didn't have the energy to move. I told Daryl to please talk to the people and handle the business for me because I couldn't even think straight. My speech was completely slurred at this point and I was ready to get to the hospital. I could see Daryl in there hurrying the man up and when he got back in the van which I struggled to get in, he looked at me slumped down and said, "Trisha, you okay?" Suddenly I couldn't talk at all. I didn't answer him I just gave half a nod. "Trisha, stay with me!"

He took off like a racecar driver and I could feel the mobility of my arm leaving me as I continued to slump further as if I was rolling up into a ball. I heard Margo say, "Honey, slow down, you're going really fast," Daryl snapped back at her in frustration, "Let me drive Margo, I've got this!" I chuckled to myself because they sounded like a typical married couple in a crisis and I'm sure Tony and I would have had the same tension given the situation, but because I know how much they love each other, I knew this moment would pass quickly.

We arrived at the hospital and I saw several paramedics rush out with a wheelchair and they opened my door and put me in it while throwing a barrage of questions my way. "What's your name?" "When's your birthday?" "Where do you live?" I was still stuck on question one and I tried to say "Trisha" but my mouth nor my tongue wanted to cooperate with my brain. Nothing came out and I was shouting, "Trisha! Trisha Mann-Grant!" in my head. That moment right there had to be the scariest thing I've experienced in a long time. It made me have a completely new love, compassion and understanding for people who are paralyzed and those who can't speak.

I sat in that wheelchair and I prayed to God from the very depths of my heart and soul. "Lord, please, I beg you, don't let me end up like my Uncle Narahjan who had a stroke five years earlier, and is still paralyzed and can't talk. Please Jesus heal me now." I was whisked inside the emergency room, clothes stripped off and hooked up to another EKG machine so fast I barely remember it all happening.

There was an IV stuck in one arm and blood being drawn from the other. The paramedics tried the questioning game again. "Can you tell us your name?" "Trisha", "Trisha!" I finally managed to get out.

Tears welled up in my eyes as my tongue broke free and I could speak. I began to sob. I knew at that moment that God heard my prayer and I was so grateful to my Heavenly Father for having mercy on me that day. I was admitted to the hospital for further tests and observation and my pastor, Pastor Arlan Sanchez came and prayed for me. My friend Alexis came and prayed for me and anointed me with her blessed oil. Margo and Daryl stayed as long as they could and they prayed too. I think I had some more visitors, but I honestly can't remember. The most important visitor came around 11 p.m. that night, my husband, Tony.

He and his entire cast had already been pre-warned by their boss, Mr. Tyler Perry himself, that no one was to leave the city while they were filming. My husband risked his job and jumped on a plane for his hardheaded wife the minute he got word that I was in the hospital. He told me later that before he left TP Studios that his fellow cast members said the most amazing and heartfelt prayer for me. I felt his presence moments before I saw him stick that beautiful, baldhead into the room. I looked up at the door seconds before he entered and I felt like a sickly,

bedridden version of Julia Roberts in the movie *Pretty Woman* when Richard Gere's character came to get her at the end.

Okay, my apologies if you haven't seen the film and I just ruined the end, but considering the movie is over twenty-five years old, cut me some slack on this one. Tony said, "I'm here to take you back to Atlanta with me so I can take care of you and nurse you back to health." That was my 'Damsel being rescued by her Prince' moment and I felt truly loved. I still tear up at the memory of him coming to get me. He spent the night in the hospital and I was released the next morning. Then the series of panic attacks started.

The following day, Tony and I had just pulled up to the airport when my first post-stroke panic, or as some refer to, anxiety attack occurred. Tony got a young lady who worked at the airport to get me a wheelchair because I was dizzy and breathing fast. I couldn't control it. At first, she thought I was faking so she was not very nice and just stared at me with this blank look. Tony said he was close to saying something when he saw her checking my hair for a weave while she was standing over me. "What's wrong with you?" she finally blurted out in a non-compassionate way. I could hardly talk but I managed to get the words, "Think-having-panic attack" out. I had experienced one of these many years ago, so it was familiar.

She said, "Well you better hurry up and get over it if you want them to let you on this plane." As I went through the process of the attack, she softened a bit from realizing that I wasn't putting on an act, and she helped me make it through check-in then wheeled me to the gate with a bit of pleasant conversation. When Tony and I reached the gate, and sat down waiting to hear our group number for boarding, I had another attack. He looked at me and said, "Baby, they're not going to let you on this plane if they see you going through this so look at me." I stared in his eyes as I was having difficulties breathing. "Keep looking in my eyes, I got you, it's going to be alright. Calm down." His voice was soothing me and I began to relax. It was time to board the plane. While walking to my seat, I could feel another attack flaring up. I quickly sat down and faced the window so the flight attendant didn't see me.

I didn't know at the time that this was a normal post response from having a stroke. Some people deal with depression and anxiety after a stroke. The idea of both simultaneously was more than I wanted to deal with and I thought to myself, "How am I going to finish writing my book in this condition?" Tony did the, "Look in my eyes" method once again, it helped, and we prayed as we always do before we take off in the air. I managed to make it through the entire flight without another attack until we landed and then another one hit.

He took me to our favorite seafood restaurant in Atlanta, Spondivits, and I had pep in my step as we approached the place. They have the best crab legs and the thought of them makes my mouth water. We sat down at the bar area because as always Spondivits is packed and then it happened, another panic attack, right there at the bar. I was starting to get a little irritated with these frequent unexpected "situations" and at the possibility of my crab leg experience being disrupted. Once again, Tony calmed me down as the bartender noticed and asked me if I was okay.

I prayed it wouldn't happen any more so I could eat in peace and God heard my prayer. Once the crab legs came, I felt like I had been cured. That would only last until we got to our hotel. While outside in the car, another attack and then another one inside the room and it seemed like every half an hour or less, *here we go again*. Even if I received a stressful phone call, I had another one. My son called, asking if I would put him on my car insurance and that triggered an attack. The simplest things that usually wouldn't faze me would send me into these nonstop episodes, so Tony shut the phone down and demanded I do nothing but rest. He wouldn't even let me watch certain things on television if they seemed to upset me.

I rested for a full week and each day the attacks came less and less but they kept coming daily. At the end of the week and a serious condition of cabin fever, I went to the TP Studios with Tony on their final shoot day of *Love Thy Neighbor*, Mr. Perry didn't fire him for leaving town, thank God; in fact, he was very understanding and genuinely concerned about my health. I appreciated his kindness and the love from all the cast members. I am also grateful to Palmer, Patrice, Darmirra, Kendra, Andre, Leigh Ann, and Jonathan for the love and support they showed my husband and the prayers sent up for me. Months later, I was down to one or two attacks a day, but it was still frustrating.

I would do my testimonies for this book from home in the bed and every once in a while, I would get brave enough to actually meet with someone and sit down for an Amazing Testimony interview.

Other than that, most of the interviews were done on the phone but the spirit of procrastination still hit me from time to time stopping me from being diligent and productive. For instance, even though this is Chapter 2, I've completed most of this book and I am just now entering this story.

One month later, after once again getting "back on the horse" and tackling my mission, I had severe back spasms hit me out of nowhere. It was physically debilitating and I couldn't think about doing anything because I was in constant pain. The slightest movement would trigger a spasm and it felt like someone was stabbing me with quick, deep, hard jabs everywhere. The spasms came as often as the panic attacks when I first started having them. God forbid, I had a spasm and a panic attack at the same time. My children were so concerned about me and they sometimes had to help me in or out of the bed.

I thought often, *Lord, what in the world is going on with me?* My business consultant Hugh sent me some back exercises to do and in the beginning, they were excruciating but I pushed through the pain and it started to help. Then my son Daniel said, "Mom, I want you to go to Bible study with me. Lovey (his Bible study teacher) has the gift of healing and he can pray over your panic attacks." It sounded like a good idea to me, so we went. At the end of Bible study, everyone was pulling at the anointed young man and I managed to get his attention for a second. I told him about the stroke and the anxiety and he laid hands on my head and said a very short quick prayer, then he looked at me and said, "You will have no more panic attacks in Jesus Name, amen." I thanked him and then he moved on to the next person.

I was honestly looking for something a lot more spectacular to take place. I wanted to say, "That's it, Brother? Can we go in just a little bit longer?" But I received the prayer and then believed the prayer. I can tell you that I haven't had a panic attack since the day that young man laid hands on me. I have experienced flutters from time to time in my chest but I thank God for healing me and restoring my body even from the back spasms.

Many moons ago when my children were very young, I was healed from depression as well. Depression is like the Black Hole in space, taking you deeper until you spiral downward fast, sucking you in. You wake up in the mornings and don't have the energy to get out of bed. There is no drive or ambition alive inside of you and every second feels like an hour. You go through the motions just to get through the day like a functioning zombie and your self-worth has lost its meaning and value. It was hard enough for me to take care of myself, but I was a single mother with depression caring for two little children. I knew I could not remain in that state of mind any longer, which left me feeling hopeless and worthless, so I literally forced myself to pray during my depression and then one day I sat on my couch with my Bible on my lap and the thought of opening it was exhausting. It took everything in me to open that Bible and when I did, the first thing I read sent a surge of power through my body and I instantly felt refreshed, renewed, and restored. I have not suffered from depression since, thank God! The act of opening God's Word was an act of submission and faith. When you combine prayer and faith, the outcome is always something supernatural and miraculous. I am a walking AMAZING TESTIMONY.

Speak Life Into Your Life.

AMAZING TESTIMONY
by:
TONY GRANT
Actor/Singer from Tyler Perry's LOVE THY NEIGHBOR on OWN
and many stage productions
Former member of the R & B group AZYET
Album: ACCESS GRANTED
Instagram: @tgrant621

LOVE NEVER TOLD

On the day I made the decision to tell my grandfather that I loved him for the very first time, he had a fatal heart attack working outside in the field. I was fifteen years old when my grandfather passed away and I didn't eat for a couple of weeks because I never told him I loved him.

I was trying to do anything to take away the pain of my mourning. I went out and played ball in 100-degree weather in Polk County, North Carolina with the humidity making it 120 degrees. I was not caring how hot it was nor caring about my health, so as a result, I fell out. My whole left side shut down.

I had a mild stroke. For five or six months, I couldn't speak clearly, but only from the right side of my mouth. The muscles on my left side had totally stopped working. I prayed about it and told God I wanted to speak and I didn't want to look deformed. I laid hands on myself and prayed and when I looked in the mirror the very next day, all of my muscles came back to normal.

I didn't know a whole lot about Faith, I just knew about praying. I touched my face and said, "God, you're going to heal me because I know you don't want me like this for the rest of my life."

During that five to six-month period, I was in a state of depression and spent most of the time feeling sorry for myself. I remember some of the kids at school were laughing at me. I thought I was being punished because I didn't tell my Grandfather I loved him before he died.

37

After being completely restored, it took me years to realize that keeping my mouth shut was a huge mistake and you must speak what's on your heart because pride can cause you to be too late.

Tomorrow is not promised, so be diligent in what you do today. I love you Poppa.

Sometimes God may not move your mountains but He will give you the strength to climb.

AMAZING TESTIMONY
by:
ORNETTA BARBER-WILKERSON
Former Music Executive of WEA, Inc.
(Warner Bro.'s/Elektra/Atlantic Records)
Facebook: Ornetta Barber

ORNETTA'S ANGELS

My symptoms started in 2011 when I noticed I didn't have any energy. I was winded just trying to climb the stairs. When I would get winded, I could catch my breath before, but now I felt like I was going to faint. My doctor checked me out and suggested a stress test. I went to see him a week early for my annual physical and I asked to have my blood drawn. He called me with the results that I was severely anemic and I needed to get a blood transfusion. I made an appointment for a colonoscopy, and when I woke up, they said I had a massive tumor that had to be removed. They removed it and then said I had stage three-colon cancer.

For three years prior to that, I was in a severe depression. I no longer wanted to go hang out with friends or go to parties I was invited to. I made up excuses just to stay home. Once the tumor was removed, the depression went away. The doctor said the tumor started growing in 2009 and people don't realize that some tumors can lead to depression. 2009 is when the depression started.

To fight the 'good fight' you can't be depressed so I called one of my wonderful girlfriends that had cancer from the hospital to tell her what was up. Pat Shield's, whom I hadn't talked to in over a year dropped what she was doing and came to visit me and stayed with me for over three hours. She suggested I tell the rest of our close friends via conference call what was going on and she was with me through the whole process of recovery. It was Pat's idea that we all came together for my chemo process. Pat dubbed all my friends, "Ornetta's Angels."

Each month we all did something positive together. One month we went to the beach, another we went to a restaurant, one time we went over someone's house and celebrated each other. Everyone rallied around me tremendously. My husband, mother, friends, and my nephew Billy all fought the good fight with me. I was back to being the joyful person I used to be. I went through chemo for six months twice a month and it made me feel lousy during the time I was doing chemo for four days straight each month.

My hair got very thin and I lost a lot of my eyelashes. I lost fifteen pounds and thought, *This is a hell of a way to lose some weight but I wouldn't recommend the chemo diet to anyone.* The first time I met my doctor, Karo Arzoo, he came into my room to tell me I had cancer. He leaned over my bed, looked at me, put his hand on my cheek, and said, "You have colon cancer stage three." He has been the best doctor and agreed to be my primary care doctor since I met him. My husband Bobby was also the best 'Doctor'. I called him Dr. Feel Good.

A year or two after things went by, my husband confessed that he was angry and in a dark place about what happened to me. He never showed me his frustration or any negative thoughts or feelings because he wanted me to get well. I just feel like I've always had a blessed life but the older I get and different experiences I've gone through, the more blessed I feel.

People had been there for me like my mom. She was a little spitfire, full of life, doing everything for everyone. When I first told her I had cancer, she hesitated, paused, started crying and then immediately said, "We're going to beat this. We got this."

My sister died of pancreatic cancer thirteen years ago, which is why I dreaded telling my mom because she already lost a daughter to cancer. There was a time that my sister and I had some issues and stopped talking; however, I am grateful that my beautiful sister and I were no longer estranged seven years before she passed. She was smart, funny, and talented and I'm glad we became close before her death.

A year after my diagnosis, my mom got sick. Her symptoms included lack of appetite; she was very tired all the time and she no longer desired sweets. I knew something was wrong when she didn't want her sweets anymore. She never had a weight issue but she got thin during her sickness and we had to make her eat. I prayed she would not suffer, and nine days after she went home for hospice, she passed. I lost my mom two years ago, to lung cancer.

The last week of her life, I took some movies over to my mom and she saw *Gravity* with Sandra Bullock and *Nebraska* with Bruce Stern. I told mom, "You don't need to go to the movies; I'll bring the movies to you." I also made her a custom music CD. Janis Ian's, "*At Seventeen*," was one of her favorite songs and Gladys Knight, "*Me and You Against the World*." Barbara Streisand, Lionel Richie, and Luis Miguel were also artists she listened to that last week of her life with us.

I tried to spoil her most of my adult life so there were no regrets when she passed. I always told her I loved her and she always told me she was so proud of me. I've lost a lot of people in my life, but I think about my sister every day for the last thirteen years. I celebrate her and I smile because she and my mom's spirits were so strong.

I dreamed about my mom about four weeks ago, we were laughing and then I broke down and started crying and I said, "I miss you mom," she grabbed me and hugged me in the dream and said, "Baby please, I'm good, and I haven't gone anywhere. I'm here." That dream was so vivid it felt like I was really with her. For the last twenty-three years of her life, she lived with her significant other Harry Lindeman, also known as Oom Harry, which means uncle in Dutch. He's eighty-nine and still here.

My mom had me at fifteen and was married to my daddy for three years. She left him because he was a knucklehead. He and I still had a good relationship and he had an amazing sense of humor. She married my stepfather who was a knucklehead too. Uncle Harry took her to Europe twice and Hawaii several times. Before that, she had never been out of the country. He could do anything with his hands. He was a serious Artisan with his specialty in Rod iron.

She begged me to promise her that I would watch out for him and I said I would. I go see Uncle Harry every ten to fourteen days, make food for him, take him to the park, out to lunch, and pay his bills for him. Initially I did it for Mom, but now I do it because I want to and I feel like she's happy because she asked me to do something specific and I've done it. His mind is sharp as a tack but his legs are giving out. He misses Mom so much just like the rest of us. I send him positive mantras via email and he looks forward to my visits. It makes me so happy to know that this man brought her joy and treated her like a queen.

41

Through my sickness, I never felt like I was going to die even though chemo was hard. Food had no flavor and I wore a pouch that administered chemo to me through a port that was put through my upper left chest. My nurses and staff were wonderful and I called them my 'Fusion Angels.' The room I went in to get chemo was called the fusion room so that's how they got their name. This went on for two days twice a month for six months.

I never felt like it was a death sentence because I had faith and I believed God still had work for me to do and God wouldn't take two of my mom's daughters away from her making her go through that pain twice. I didn't even think I would go through that type of experience twice but I did with my mom and Sister. I dwell on all the good things about both of them and post those positive messages on Facebook.

Now I only have to go to the doctor twice a year and the diagnosis is that I'm in remission doing great and I see him again next month for my first visit. Next year, I will just be doing my annual visit but I feel wonderful and I know that having the right doctor is very important. I thank God I have that.

I would say to anyone going through this to keep the faith and have a positive attitude, even if you're not a believer. You can't fight the good fight and have a funky attitude. Some people say, "Why me," I say, "Why not me? What makes me so special that I can't experience it?"

Eliminate negative energy from your life and be surrounded by positive thinking people. The world is very dark right now. We need some light and we all can shed a little light on others, strangers, and all. You never know how you can touch a person with kind words and deed. Have a good support system and pay it forward.

AMAZING TESTIMONY
by:
TONY GRANT
Actor/Singer from Tyler Perry's LOVE THY NEIGHBOR on OWN
and many stage productions.
Former member of the R & B group AZYET
Album: ACCESS GRANTED
anthonygrant22@gmail.com

BROKEN

It was 1989 and I was playing street ball with some young brothers I knew from church. I went up for a dunk and one of the guys who tried to defend me jumped at the same time I did. He landed first and my right foot landed on top of his foot. At that point, my ankle rolled over and it was so severe that my bone came through my skin.

I didn't realize what had happened until I saw that no one was trying to help me up but instead everyone ran and scattered away from me. Then I looked down at my ankle and saw that the bottom of my foot was facing the inner side of my other ankle.

After physically seeing it, the pain rushed in like a welder's torch.

No one touched me until the ambulance arrived. The paramedics couldn't stabilize my foot so the ride to the hospital was unbearable. Once I arrived, I was taken to the critical floor where they gave me pain medicine that didn't work. My whole body was now throbbing in excruciating pain.

As I listened to the doctors discussing my situation, I heard one say, "We may need to amputate because his ligaments will never repair correctly." I overheard another doctor say, "He'll never walk again." At that moment, I began to panic and have an anxiety attack because the drugs were kicking in and I could hear the voice of the Devil talking to me saying, "You will never walk again. You will never play drums again. You will never play ball again because they're going to cut off your foot."

I got angry at the voice and proclaimed, "I am going to walk!" I began to pray and God heard my prayers because the doctors put me to sleep, straightened my ankle, and put a cast on my foot up to my knee, which was supposed to stay on for three months. I stayed in the hospital for two or three days in ICU.

Once I went home, sadness came over me because no one came to visit me or call and see how I was doing for almost a month. I became depressed and the negative voices got stronger as I closed myself off in my room to lay helpless in the bed with my foot elevated.

My grandmother would come in from time to time to check on me. One particular day, she asked me if I wanted to walk. I said, "Yes, ma'am, I do." She said, "I don't believe you." Then she turned and walked out of the room. The next day, she came in to check on me and asked me again, "Do you want to walk?" and with an annoyed tone, I said, "Yes."

My grandmother stood there, looked at me in my face, and said, "No you don't." Again, she turned and walked out. The next day, here she comes again and I was ready for the question this time but I got pissed that she asked me again. Emphatically I said, "Yes!" She said, "Okay, now I believe you."

She walked over, laid hands on my ankle, and began to pray. In her prayer, I felt the presence of God and the peace of knowing I was going to walk. At night, I visibly saw myself walking.

One Sunday morning, after everyone had gone to church, I grabbed my crutches and made my way outside down the stairs of the front porch to the side of the house where my grandfather kept his tools. I grabbed his hedge clippers and went back in the house. I sat down on the couch and I told God, "I believe you want me to walk again, so by faith, I'm going to cut this cast off and I'm going to church."

By faith, I cut the cast off of my foot. The same intensity of pain that I had when I first broke my ankle came back. Because of faith and determination, I could push past the pain. I threw my crutches on the floor, grabbed my grandmother's cane, got in my car, and drove to church. When I got to church, service was already in progress and as I opened the front doors, everything came to a standstill. Everyone quietly watched me walk all the way down to the first pew. My Grandmother gave me her familiar nod of approval that she would usually give me when she approved of my singing. I stood there with feelings of gratification, happiness, and victory over the negative voices and everyone that doubted I would ever walk again.

From that day, twenty-six years ago, until now, I have never had any pain or discomfort in that ankle. I still play the drums and will take young boys to school on the basketball court. Looking back on my first defining moment of faith, I learned a very valuable lesson that I apply to my life daily; Faith is the ultimate key to my success and FAITH without WORKS is dead. Amen.

If you find a path with no obstacles, it probably doesn't lead anywhere.

- Frank A. Clark

AMAZING TESTIMONY
by:
PASTOR JEANIE GODFREY
Faith Chapel Deliverance Center
Chicago, Illinois

FORGIVE THEM, FORGIVE ME

When I woke on the morning of January 11, 2011, I had the eeriest feelings going all over my body, especially on my right side. It took me a little longer than usual to arise, but I did. All day I did not feel like my normal joyful self, but I faked it.

The next day was no better and for the next two or three days, matters seemed to be getting worse. Finally, on January 15, 2011 (I know it was this date because that is Dr. Martin Luther King, Jr.'s birthday and I honor his legacy) things had gone all the way down.

I do not check my body daily for changes so I did not notice that my right leg had swollen up to be as large as a full-grown tree trunk. Long story short, I went to the doctor, immediate hospitalization and my diagnosis was a blood clot right side. I had complete bed rest under hospital incarceration for nineteen days!

Since the time, I came home on February 2, 2011, only having a limp from the trauma to the right side, I have learned even more to be grateful to God for taking care of his unthinking children like me.

I have not always been a praise person. In fact, there was a time that I was a 'hell-raisin' person. I married my first husband when I was sixteen years of age. My husband was six years older than me and my family was not happy he had snatched a baby.

I thought marriage was 'Until death do you part'. Well, that husband taught me that marriage is until the other woman wants you and your inner self says, "Go!" It did not matter that we had three children. It wasn't of concern to him that we were trying to buy a home and the bills were severely exorbitant. It

only mattered that the unyoked female was calling him and he answered!

I had never had a cigarette, a drink, nor been in a tavern, until a year after that divorce.

Unfortunately, the friends I chose after the breakup were not the right people to keep me in the path of righteousness. I was raised in the church and had a most devout, Holy Ghost filled mother. She was what every woman should strive to be. She was kind, considerate, compassionate; yet stern, disciplined, and religious.

She raised seven boys and two girls as a single Mother; each of us had no reason to feel neglected for receiving her love. My mother, of course, was not pleased with my new choice to turn to a riotous life. She warned me there were dangers and my children needed their mother.

I didn't listen. I felt, *she doesn't want me to have any fun!* At the age of twenty-two, I had my first drink. I remember it was a smooth tasting bourbon and coke and I liked it!

The years after that first drink gave me days of torture, hurt, drunkenness, physical abuse, tongue poisoned with all kinds of four letter words, promiscuousness, and with all this, I was working weekly as an Administrative Secretary.

I had no problem going from male to male. I felt, *If one Mother's son didn't provide it, another one would*! I neglected my children tremendously, but my mother was always there picking up the slack. I provided financially but did not give love and proper affection, as a mother should. The years of sin were so many and too many.

Finally, in February 1985, I told myself, "Jeanie, enough is enough! Straighten yourself up before you'll be straightened out in a casket!" Around February 6, 1985 (I'm almost sure of the day but positive of the month and year), the Lord was kind enough to answer my cry of repentance.

Since He saved me, I have tried to live a life that is an example to others that God can save a whore, an alcoholic, a wayward, negligent mother and anyone else who wants to be changed!

My walk with God has been a pleasure, yet it had and still does have pitfalls! In the beginning, I was anxious to please everybody. It took a lot of hurt, negative comments, ugly looks, and lonely nights for me to realize, *You can't please the whole world.* You have to make sure you keep your sanity and the rest will fall in place.

The one incident I will never forget is when I was on the phone talking to a person that I had really taken to be a 'bosom buddy'. The things I was telling her were truly confidential. Less than a week later, another one of our acquaintances that I really didn't 'dig' was sitting with me in a meeting at church. She turned to me and asked a very personal question. In fact, it was about the incident I had confided to my buddy.

Later, when I asked my friend had she mentioned the conversation to the other person, she quickly told me, "Jean, you are no better than anyone else. You expect everything you say to be goody-two-shoe!"

You cannot imagine the hurt this caused me. I cried, I prayed and I wondered what to do. I even went to our Pastor and she was of no comfort. I felt the friend had also told her my secret.

To this day, I still feel angry and hurt when I mention this incident because it was the most crucial one I faced at that time. God brought me through it but it wasn't fun.

When my mother passed away, there was a two-year period of family ugliness. Two of my brothers sued me thinking Mother had left me some money. Until I was able to HEAR the Lord tell me, *I was human just like them,* I had to forgive. The situation was still not resolved.

When I finally knew the Lord was speaking, I began to ask Him to help me forgive them. When I truly forgave them, God allowed the case to be thrown out of court! My journey with the Lord has been good and I have never felt it was not worth the struggle.

When the Bishop of our church passed away in March 2003, the church honored me with Temporary Status as Pastor. I have been a member since 1985 of Faith Chapel Deliverance Center in Chicago, IL. I was installed to the position of Pastor on October 18, 2003!

The church is a small congregation, but my theme is, "We are a small church serving a BIG GOD!"

The anointing of God is what keeps me happy! Despite the limp that I still have in my right foot, there is not a thing wrong anywhere else to hinder me from praising God! I know He smiles when I make some of my requests because I talk to Him just like I talk to you and anyone else. I speak out loud! I cry! I laugh! I give myself away and let Him take over! Whenever I meditate to receive His holy messages, I do not lean on my own thoughts. It is so good to feel the comfort and warmth the Spirit gives.

If there is anyone who desires to serve the Lord, tell them to ask me how to get right with Him and stay right with Him. There is always room at the cross for one more!

If it is you who needs to bow there, feel free to come! His arms are open to receive you!

If we really want to love, we must learn how to forgive.

-Mother Theresa

SCRIPTURES ABOUT
HEALING AND FAITH

[32] *That evening after sunset the people brought to Jesus all the sick and demon-possessed.* [33] *The whole town gathered at the door,* [34] *and Jesus healed many who had various diseases. He also drove out many demons, but he would not let the demons speak because they knew who he was.*
Mark 1:32-34

[22] *Then they brought him a demon-possessed man who was blind and mute, and Jesus healed him, so that he could both talk and see.* [23] *All the people were astonished and said, "Could this be the Son of David?"*
Matthew 12:22-23

[8] *In Lystra there sat a man who was lame. He had been that way from birth and had never walked.* [9] *He listened to Paul as he was speaking. Paul looked directly at him, saw that he had faith to be healed* [10] *and called out, "Stand up on your feet!" At that, the man jumped up and began to walk.*
Acts 14:8-10

[43] *And a woman was there who had been subject to bleeding for twelve years, but no one could heal her.* [44] *She came up behind him and touched the edge of his cloak, and immediately her bleeding stopped.* [45] *"Who touched me?" Jesus asked. When they all denied it, Peter said, "Master, the people are crowding and pressing against you."* [46] *But Jesus said, "Someone touched me;" I know that power has gone out from me.* [47] *Then the woman, seeing that she could not go unnoticed, came trembling and fell at his feet. In the presence of all the people, she told why she had touched him and how she had been instantly healed.* [48] *Then he said to her, "Daughter, your faith has healed you. Go in peace."*
Luke 8:43-48

51

Now faith is the substance of things hoped for and the evidence of things not seen.

CHAPTER 3

DREAMS, VISIONS, AND MIRACLES

The earliest dream I can remember was at the age of five and it was a short one but it seemed so real. In the dream, my mother asked me to go into her room and get her cigarettes off of the dresser. When I turned on the light, the light looked like a scary female clown with arms and a very demonic face. It had a creepy voice and it was grabbing at me. The dream was so real that when I woke up I didn't want to go in my mother's room for a long time. I dreaded every time I heard, "Trisha, go in my room and get my cigarettes." I still vividly remember the way that thing looked all these years later. Maybe that's one of the reasons why I don't like cigarettes and don't smoke today.

I used to have déjà vu often as a teenager, almost daily to the point that it became normal for me to experience something very familiar. However, one night I had a dream that manifested the exact same way I dreamt it days later. At fifteen, I worked at Baskin Robbins on 87th Street in Chicago and I would walk home to 93rd Street sometimes if I didn't have a ride or someone to walk with me, but usually not at night.

In this dream, it was very dark, I had just gotten off from work, and I didn't have anyone to walk home with me. There was an eerie vibe in the atmosphere and it felt as if I was being watched or followed as I walked down certain blocks. Several nights later after the dream, I left work later than usual, it was very dark, and as I was walking, the dream instantly came back to me because I was experiencing the same path, trees, cars, and houses that I saw in the dream. I also felt that same eeriness so I walked swiftly, looked around often, prayed, and hurried home. If someone was following me, they would have had to run just to keep up and as paranoid as I was being, they definitely would have been spotted.

I know with dreams comes information or warnings so I definitely took that one as a warning. I've had quite a few prophetic dreams. One time I dreamed that my friend was in a

53

camper with her family on a road trip and it caught on fire. She called me the next day and told me that she and her children went on a trip in a camper and it caught on fire. I have had other dreams about both of my children before I knew I was pregnant and saw their Father's other children in dreams as well. I told my son's father years ago, about a baby boy I saw, he said, "Who told you she was pregnant?" I told him that I saw a slightly younger, lighter complexion version of our baby, sitting right next to our son on a bunk bed dressed in the same clothes but different colors. I told him it was a dream but my intuition told me that he was going to have another child soon and six months after our conversation, he had a son with that exact description.

I dreamed about my daughter's other brother as well but it was not the same type of dream, I did know in my spirit that it was a boy and he was close to her age. Even after seeing my own children in dreams, the news of my daughter surprised me most because I thought that she would come here way down the road and not under the circumstances in which I experienced that pregnancy. That story is highlighted in Chapter 9.

A month before I found out I was pregnant with my son; my deceased grandmother and deceased Uncle Robby came to me in a vision to tell me about Daniel. They simply walked through my grandmother's front door, walked up to me where I was sitting on her living room floor and they said, "You're going to have a little boy, he is going to be very special. Whatever you do, don't get an abortion." They walked out of the door just as quickly as they entered and the vision was over.

It wasn't until I found out I was pregnant that the memory of the vision came back to me and I was obedient to my uncle and grandmother. Before my grandmother passed when I was 21, my uncle died of a blood clot that rose to his heart from a broken ankle two years earlier. He was like a big brother to me and I had seen many of my relatives pass away and even sang at many of their funerals, but I think my grandmother and I both took Uncle Robby's death very hard.

One night after his death, Uncle Robby came to me in a dream just like he would do a few years later to give me information about my son. He said, "Trish, Mama's going to die a day from now." I shook my head and started to cry and he continued, "Get ready, she is going to die."

A week later, I woke up abruptly at 6 a.m. and I had a strong feeling to go downstairs. Once I got downstairs into the living room, I saw Granny lying on the couch and I knew in my spirit that something was wrong. She had vomit coming from her mouth and she couldn't move but she was breathing. I didn't know it then but she had, had a stroke. I called my mother who called the ambulance. I told my mother, "Mom, I think this is it." She said, "So do I baby." When the paramedics came to get Granny, I walked in the living room from the kitchen and saw them looking at each other. The female paramedic was shaking her head at the man as if to say, "This one's not gonna make it." I told them I was going to put on some jeans and be right down so I could ride with her in the ambulance.

When I came back downstairs, they had put her in the ambulance and through the big picture window in the living room, I could see them taking off down the street. I was so angry that they didn't say something and angrier that I wasn't in that ambulance with her. It took me years to get over that anger toward the paramedics but as I matured, I realized that she needed to be rushed to the hospital immediately.

When I finally arrived, and got a chance to see her for the last time, I heard her whispering, "Stand by me Jesus, stand by me." I bent down and whispered in her ear, "I love you Granny." She managed to respond, "I love you too." I didn't know at that moment that those would be the last words I would hear my grandmother say. Hours later, the family decided to go home because it was late and many of my aunts, uncles, and cousins were at her house.

Everyone was talking and I sat on the stairway quietly feeling an enormous amount of sadness when the phone rang. I knew with every fiber of my being that it was the hospital and that my best friend was gone. I reluctantly answered, "Hello," "Yes, hi, this is Nurse__calling from South Chicago Hospital about Ruth Randall." "Yes, she is my grandmother." "I am sorry to inform you that your grandmother has expired." I thought to myself, *who uses a term like expire in regards to someone passing away? My grandmother is not a carton of milk!*

My mom and the rest of the family immediately went to the hospital to say our proper goodbyes to Granny. The walk down the hallway to her room seemed like a mile and in my mind, I was determined to be strong for my mother. As we reached the corner of the door and I saw my grandmother's body lying still

on that hospital bed, my legs turned into noodles, buckled underneath me and I hit the floor sobbing. They took me into a room where I cried for hours it seemed. God allowed my Uncle Robby to come to me in a vision to soften the blow and give me a warning of my grandmother's death because He knew how much I loved her and how hard I would take it.

I am grateful for all of the dreams and visions I have ever received over the years. It is important to write them down and date them because our wonderful human brains can sometimes forget the most important details; details that may help us later down life's road.

And still, after all this time, the sun never says to the earth,

"You owe me." Look what happens with a love

like that, it lights the whole sky.

- Hafez

AMAZING TESTIMONY
by:
IMANI NAKIA DUDLEY
Dancer/Choreographer
Instagram: @coolbrezzee

THE KING OF POP

My first memory of Michael Jackson was when I was sitting in front of the television at the age of four watching him in his famous black suit with white socks dancing in the music video, *Billy Jean*. It would be almost four years later that I would gain an interest in dancing myself. I was fascinated with the talents and artistry of Michael Jackson and I admired him and loved what he stood for. It was his heart that intrigued me most. He seemed to be a very giving and generous person. I consistently watched his videos over and over and practiced his dance moves hoping I would one day captivate an audience the way he captivated me.

On a cold Detroit night in January of 2009, I had a very disturbing dream that seemed more real than dream-like about the King of Pop, Michael Jackson. In the dream, I was in my bed at home watching a show on television and the words, BREAKING NEWS came across the screen and the reporter said, "The King of Pop was rushed to the hospital and pronounced dead."

When I woke up I was very shaken and it was difficult to go back to sleep. I didn't know what to do. I was afraid to mention the dream to anyone because it was so real but eventually I told my sister and she was shocked too. She said, "You need to pray for him." I did. I prayed for his health, healing and for God's will to be done.

In 2008, I had a similar experience when I dreamed about my grandmother's death so this felt very familiar. In my dream about my grandmother I received a phone call where the person on the other end whom I recall was my uncle said, "Nana died." I was just as shaken from awaking after this dream. My cousin's boyfriend reached out to me that next week to tell me that Nana was sick. The doctors said she had a lump in her breast that they thought was cancerous. Once again, I had told my sister the dream and she told me to pray for Nana. I did and we went to visit her and prayed for her while we held her hand. She accepted Jesus again in her heart and even though the doctors gave her six months to live, God blessed us to have her for three more years.

I hoped that by praying for Michael Jackson as I did for Nana that we would have him longer so my dream would not come to pass. However, six months after my very real dream about M.J., he passed on June 25, 2009. I was driving and the deejay announced that Michael Jackson was rushed to the hospital and I was immediately reminded of my dream back in January. I was freaked out and I went home right away. The minute I turned on the television it said, BREAKING NEWS and everything I experienced in my dream unfolded before my eyes.

Almost six months later, I was asked to dance in an amazing tribute to Michael Jackson at The Music Hall in Detroit. It was an emotional performance for me and I was still in shock that he was gone. I danced my heart out in remembrance of one of my favorite artists and humanitarians. Michael Jackson will forever make me look at the *"Man in the Mirror."*

You were created to make somebody else's life better. Somebody needs your smile. They need your love, your encouragement and your gifts.

- Joel Osteen

AMAZING TESTIMONY
by:
TOI L'ECHE NOLEN-SMITH
KING TOI
Facebook: Toi L'eche Nolen-Smith

FEAR NO EVIL

I have been awoken by angels giving me direction on what was going to happen in certain churches, revivals, conferences and the different spirits and demons I would face there. In Arizona, I had prayer sessions where my friend Terry would come to my house and pray with me. One day, the Lord showed me that my sister was in a relationship with a voodoo priest and as I was praying in the "Great Room" for my sister to be released from this relationship, a giant anaconda snake projected himself in the glass.

I called my mom and said, "Who is this man my sister is seeing?" She said, "How did you know?" I told my mom to go where this man was, take a drop of anointed oil and drop it on the floor and there would be two men sitting in chairs and the man would have a necklace of an upside-down Star of David, she was already invited by the man to come so she said, "How do you know I will get in and be able to do this?" I said, "I just know, just drop the oil."

She went and saw the two men sitting at the table playing cards and then my sister's boyfriend, the voodoo priest, came out wearing the necklace with the star of David. After she dropped the oil, we went back into prayer to cast him out. This time he came back as the snake and tried to project himself through the glass, but the prayers were too powerful. Thank God my sister broke up with the witch a few days later and we never heard from him again or heard anything about him. The same girlfriend, Terry who prayed for my sister with me is the one I was going to one of the church revivals with in Tucson, we were each others Armor Bearers but there was a lot of witchcraft in that area.

59

We got there and there were a lot of demonic entities, witchcraft, and voodoo. We went home after the second night of services and I was the only one to stay awake and the Angel of the Lord said, *"I need you to stay awake, I need to show you something,"* I said, "Prove yourself to me Angel so I know that it's you." So, he gave me a scripture and song in my heart. The song, *"His Eye Is On The Sparrow"* and the scripture, Hebrews 11:1, *"Now faith is the substance of things hoped for and the evidence of things not seen."*

As a prophet, the Lord taught me, that pleading the Blood of Jesus is sufficient to say when an angel appears to you. I don't need to know who the spirit is, if it is not of God it has to go. This was definitely an Angel of the Lord. As I sat there in April's prayer room, suddenly I saw people jumping out of windows in the spirit realm, Angels flying all over the place, fire trucks, police cars, Angels in buildings, on top of buildings, kneeling on the ground near people, carrying people. There were planes, smoke and massive chaos. The Angel said, "Pack, tell the story and get out or you will be stuck. Go home to your family."

Everyone was sleep and I started packing my bags. They laughed at me when I told them the story. They told me I was crazy, I called and told my husband to get me out of here right now it's urgent. Two singers heard my vision and they were very afraid, April and Terry told me I was crazy and they were each a prophetess! April was a thirty-year-old virgin prophetess who had witches and warlocks in her church so she was constantly praying and giving others prophecy. These other girls, the singers, did not know me, but they listened.

I got home the next day, my husband called me and said, "Baby, I need you to turn on the news right now." I sat down on my bed turned on the news and the World Trade Center had been bombed. I had to keep Terry's nine-month old baby for about a week because she was stranded in Arizona. She never questioned me again. April stayed in Tucson and closed her ministry doors about a year later, but I have not spoken to her since 9/11. I told everyone around me and they all except two laughed or didn't believe me. I wish I could find those two singers who did listen to the warning. I wonder how they are doing. I am grateful I have learned always to listen to my first mind, which is my spirit man.

AMAZING TESTIMONY
by:
TONY TOPAZ
Filmmaker
www.dollarperview.com

DEATH WATCH

About seven years ago, I discovered that I had a mysterious issue with blood clots called Deep Vein Thrombosis. I was back and forth in the hospital over twenty different times because of this ailment. It felt like a Charlie horse in my legs and sometimes prevented me from being able to walk without enduring a severe limp. Sometimes I couldn't walk at all without the use of crutches. I soon realized this was a result of many blood clots forming that broke off and ran up into my chest.

On one particular stay at the hospital after the doctors learned the severity of the blood clots spreading, I was told that I was going to be put on Death Watch. They said, "There is a strong chance that you will not survive through the night."

The doctors had tried to thin my blood clots and ordered me to lie in bed and be very still so the medication could work properly. They also wanted me to use a bedpan so I wouldn't stand up, but I replied, "If I'm going to die, it's going to be with dignity and not with a pan up my butt."

Shortly after they left, their words sunk in and I could see and hear the heart machine next to me. The doctors said frankly, "You are like a time bomb. Once the blood clots hit your heart, there is nothing we can do. No surgery will help. It will be instant death."

They then asked me, "If you do survive, would you be willing to stay on life support if you were brain dead?" I declined life support because I have never feared death. We are all going at some point.

I began to think about my children and how I wanted them to be okay and how I wanted to finish the many things I had

started with my career, so the stress about dying and not leaving something behind and unfinished bothered me. My desire was to leave my mark in this world that would leave a legacy to help support my children.

I did the opposite of what the doctors requested and went for a walk in the Hospital, Mercy Gilbert, as I was walking I saw the hospital sign logo on the floor below me in a circle. MERCY was on the top and GILBERT was on the bottom. As I stood there staring at the sign, it glinted and the MERCY part of the sign glowed bright on the floor, the first part of the sign, shining only on the MERCY part.

The minute I saw this I knew I would be fine. The next morning all the doctors came in scratching their heads and they said, "we can't really explain this, but every one of the clots in your chest are gone. We don't know what's going on here?" In my head, I thought, *I do. It's a miracle.*

They sent me home that following day. That was God's way of letting me know it was not my time to go home to the place He has prepared for me yet. Life is about living and loving what you do and now seven years later, I have a chance to do just that.

You've gotta dance like there's nobody watching, love like you'll never be hurt, sing like there's nobody listening,
and live like it's Heaven on earth.
-William W. Purkey

AMAZING TESTIMONY
by:
HUSSEIN MANN
Writer
Facebook: Hussein Mann
Instagram: @husseinmann

LET IT BE OKAY

My second ex-wife and I were in our old four-door Sedan and she was driving down the street in the suburbs. I was unaware that we were moments away from having what would be our second car accident one year later.

The first car accident happened while we were in the midst of an argument. At that time, she was my girlfriend and she was dropping me off at work. We were discussing my issues with her ex-boyfriend still hanging around and the next thing I knew, my upper body was flying half way through the windshield before I was violently thrown back into the seat. She broke one of the bones in her foot because it slipped underneath the brake pedal. However, she managed to get out of the car and run around it to get to me.

She grabbed me, pulled me out and sat me on the ground right next to the car with the car door open. I groggily asked, "What happened? What's going on?"

She said, "Forget and live."

I went unconscious, woke up in the hospital bed feeling a woman's arms around me. I opened my eyes and was surprised to see that it was the arms of my first ex-wife who came to check on me at the hospital. I asked her what happened, and she told me I was in a car accident and broke the windshield with my head. Immediately, I became aware of the pain in my bandaged head.

"Your girlfriend drove the car into a pillar of the railroad viaduct. Your head broke the glass windshield." She looked surprised and she sat straight up and asked me, "Don't you remember?"

That statement took my mind back to my girlfriend's statement which was "Forget and live." At that point I passed out again with her sitting on the side of the bed.

Suddenly I saw everything that happened in my life being erased right before my eyes and it sounded like a reel tape being run backward. Pictures flashed before my eyes from present time to past, second by second and for the three days I was unconscious, my mind continued to erase my past, completely.

The doctors thought I was going to die and told everyone my chances of survival weren't good. When I woke up, a young man was standing in front of me and I didn't recognize him. He said, "Don't you remember me? I'm your cousin." He looked familiar, but I couldn't recall who this person was. The nurse came to me with a bedpan and I looked confused. She looked at me, put her hand on her hip, cocked her head to the side and frowned at me as if to say, *Come on, you know what this is.*

My cousin said, "He really doesn't know what it is. He lost his memory." He offered to help me to the bathroom. He said, "There's a bathroom right here. Do you need me to help you in there?"

I instantly became aware of the pressure in my bladder. Then I walked to the bathroom and had to reacquaint myself with the fixtures in a bathroom. The shower, the sink and the toilet were all slightly familiar as well, but it was strange not knowing something that I should know.

I went back to my bed and my cousin sat down in the visitor's chair and the phone on the snack tray next to my bed rang. I looked at this box object and wondered what it was and why was it ringing? I honestly didn't know.

He said, "Aren't you going to answer the phone?"

My instincts told me to pick up the receiver. I reached for the phone and picked it up; the chord pulled downward so common sense told me to put the lower portion to my mouth and the upper part to my ear.

I was talking to a woman who seemed to know me and when she realized that I didn't recognize her she got angry and slammed the phone down in my ear. After my cousin left, I lay in bed and was keenly aware of the different sounds and smells I heard in the background and wondered what was all of that about. I felt like a newborn baby inside of a grown man's body and that was the most awkward experience of all for me. Soon, I began to receive multiple visits by various women who sat around the room sharing their stories about me and all of our relationships. I was ashamed and embarrassed that I was the person they were referring to, and even though they looked familiar, I didn't remember anything they were discussing.

Over time I slowly got my memory back. During the following year in my attempts to regain my memory, I took several self-help courses in Chicago, I prayed and ended up marrying my girlfriend and made her my second wife. She would go to church with me and she tried to help me remember everything by pushing me to do the things I was afraid of doing, like driving a car. She told me, "Driving is just like riding a bike, you never forget." She was right, but I did forget all of the traffic laws and I got a few tickets. After that, I studied the rules of the road book. Every year since that accident happened, things continuously come back to me and it feels like a spiritual revelation.

Approximately a year later around the same time as that first accident, I had regained a sufficient amount of my memory so I could lead a normal life again. This time there was no argument in the car and once again my second wife was driving because I was tired after a long day of work. I fell asleep in the car. She did not like that at all. Apparently, she blacked out, as I found out later she had blacked out when the first accident occurred, and when the car hit the curb I woke up to us crashing into a wooden power line pole on the opposite side of the sidewalk from the street and once again my head slammed into the windshield. What followed was something I have never experienced before.

I fell back into my seat and I felt warm blood running down my face. I slumped down forward on the dashboard and I went unconscious. I saw myself in a black open space with absolutely no light. I began screaming, "Not again! Not again!" I was screaming this over and over and all of a sudden, I began sliding forward as if I were on a greased wooden plank. I knew in my spirit that if I didn't stop screaming "Not again! Not again!" I would drop off of this plank into a vast void of nothingness and I would be screaming, "Not again, not again!" for the rest of eternity.

I stopped saying those words and something inside of me encouraged me to say, "Let it be okay. Let it be okay." At that moment, I lifted my head, which was laying down on the seat next to her, looked up at her and I said, "Let it be okay."

She placed her hands on my shoulders and said, "Are you okay?" "Yes," I said.

She looked at the front of the hood of the car wrapped around the wooden pole. She balled her fist and slammed it against the steering wheel.

I sat up, looked in the rear view mirror and was amazed to see that the blood had disappeared from my face. There was a one-inch wide-open gash on my forehead and it was so deep I could see the white meat behind my skin, but the strangest thing is that there was no blood coming out of it. The windshield was severely cracked from the impact of my head, but there wasn't even any blood on the windshield.

Miraculously, the wound healed in two days and on the third day it had completely disappeared. There was no sign of it. Humanly impossible but obviously not impossible with God. This experience was a true miracle.

Your expectation is the breeding ground for your miracle.

SCRIPTURES ABOUT DREAMS, VISIONS, AND MIRACLES

28 But there is a God in heaven who reveals mysteries. He has shown King Nebuchadnezzar what will happen in days to come. Your dream and the visions that passed through your mind as you were lying in bed are these.
Daniel 2:28

13 When they had gone, an angel of the Lord appeared to Joseph in a dream. "Get up," he said, "take the child and his mother and escape to Egypt. Stay there until I tell you, for Herod is going to search for the child to kill him."
Matthew 2:13

9 One night the Lord spoke to Paul in a vision: "Do not be afraid; keep on speaking, do not be silent."
Acts 18:9

9 He performs wonders that cannot be fathomed, miracles that cannot be counted.
Job 5:9

13 Simon himself believed and was baptized. And he followed Philip everywhere, astonished by the great signs and miracles he saw.
Acts 8:13

20 He replied, "Because you have so little faith. Truly I tell you, if you have faith as small as a mustard seed, you can say to this mountain, 'Move from here to there,' and it will move. Nothing will be impossible for you."
Matthew 17:20

29 Then Jesus told him, "Because you have seen me, you have believed; blessed are those who have not seen and yet have believed." 30 Jesus performed many other signs in the presence of his disciples, which are

not recorded in this book. [31] But these are written that you may believe that Jesus is the Messiah, the Son of God, and that by believing you may have life in his name.
John 20:29-31

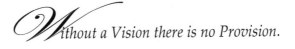
Without a Vision there is no Provision.

CHAPTER 4

NEAR DEATH EXPERIENCES

I have never had a Near Death Experience (or NDE as some refer to it), at least not that I can remember and I am sure that is not something one can easily forget unless God wants them to. I have had however, many supernatural experiences and my spirit Astral projected from my body a few times, unintentionally. I am aware of people who practice Astral projection daily, but I believe strongly that God prefers we don't practice such things because when you leave your body, any type of spirit can enter it while it is not occupied, not to mention, it is against His Will.

Also, Astral Projection can allow you to see friends and family without their knowledge. That would technically be considered invasion of privacy and a form of witchcraft. "I knew a young lady who practiced Astral Projection and found out that her boyfriend was cheating on her that way." I personally have never been attracted to such practices and I don't want to do anything that is going to lead me away from relying strictly on the guidance of the Holy Spirit.

I will discuss more about the supernatural in another book to come. Most people are afraid of that subject matter, but there are things that many need to be aware of. I do like to watch Kat Kerr's you tube videos on her visits to Heaven over the years because she is a true woman of God with a gift and anointing. She also backs up everything she teaches about Heaven with scripture. Her words are encouraging to those of us who lose a loved one and wonder what's going on in the afterlife. Bottom line, if they believed that Jesus was the Son of God, he died for our sins and was raised from the dead, they stand an amazing chance of experiencing what we know of as Heaven.

I know each of these people personally who tell their stories of how they died and returned and I believe their stories to be true.

AMAZING TESTIMONY
by:
TOI L'ECHE NOLEN-SMITH
KING TOI
Facebook: Toi L'eche Nolen-Smith
Instagram: @therealtoi88

YOU HAVE TO GO BACK

I was in Las Vegas and I was pregnant. My brother Mike had hooked up with someone from Queen Latifah's team. Word had gotten back that they wanted to meet Mike, so Tony (my husband at the time), and I had to drive him to California and this day I wasn't feeling that great and the guy never showed up. I got so angry, I started cramping really bad and I told Tony I needed to go to the emergency room because I wasn't feeling good. When we arrived at the ER they weren't picking up a heartbeat.

I saw Dr. Como and he said, "I'm not picking up a fetal heartbeat," but we saw something moving in my stomach. They called it 'Aftermath flutter'. There was a book of a woman who wrote about an NDE (Near Death Experience) and I was supposed to read it, but I didn't. They told me to have a D&C (Dilation and Curettage) because the baby was dead, but I felt like the baby was still alive. When they were prepping me for the surgery I called my mother and told her to pray for me, and that I loved her. I called Tony and said, "Do me a favor, if I die, I want your blood, no one else's blood."

A fifteen-minute D&C turned into them resuscitating me twice and then me being on life support. I recall seeing myself literally come outside of my physical body. I could see all the doctors and it was mass hysteria in that room that day because they weren't expecting that to happen. I remember the doctor talking to Tony because I was fighting for my life. I could see myself watching from above. I was in a state of levitation, hovering, I had no need to sit or take a break. I was very comfortable floating in air. It seemed to be second nature.

70

They were scrambling to keep me alive. I remember talking
to the Angel of the Lord, saying, "I like it up here, I don't have
to go back." The Angel of the Lord said, "Toi, it's not your time,
you have to go back." I said, "No I don't," he said, "Yes, you
do." I've always been feisty. Then I flat-lined. There are no
words to describe Heaven and the peace I had and the beauty
but I will try my best. It wasn't a whole all white description
that people tend to give, for me it was also like eclipse
brightness. It was very bright throughout as far as I could see. It
stretched for miles and I could see other entities but I didn't
know who they were. They were going about their day, some
were in praise and worship, and some were being called out on
assignment. They weren't going and coming through doors or
stepping downward, they traveled through a spiritual wall or
dimension. It is an indescribable beauty that I have never seen
on this earth, either through a picture or a movie. There was so
much comfort that surrounded me. I was experiencing a
playback of my life like a vision and when I got to the visual of
my family, the Angel said, "What about Tam and Tony?" I
thought to myself, *wow, what about them?* I was so enamored
with being in the presence of Heaven that the reality of them
was almost forgotten.

They let Tony come in and he said something to me, but I
can't recall and I flat-lined again. I was in between Heaven and
earth, hearing my husband's voice and talking to the Angel at
the same time. It was as though the whole purpose of the
second flat-line was for me to talk more to the Angel. I said,
"You're right, I do have to stay for Tony and Tam, but promise
me I'll have a son." I don't remember his response, but ten
years after my Near-Death Experience on November 9, 2001,
two months after 9/11 (in which God had given me a vision
about that dates events), I had a little boy, and his name is T.J.

When I came to in my hospital room, my mother was there
and she had a notepad for me to write on because I had a tube
stuck down my throat and I couldn't talk. I repeatedly wrote,
Am I gonna die again? Later that day after the nurses removed
the breathing tube, when the doctor entered, he looked at me
like he had seen a ghost. I said, "Hi Dr. Como." He was in
shock that I was sitting up, wide-awake and very alert after
dying twice.

I went back to Vegas after having my son and I went back to
visit Dr. Como to let him know I had a son and that I was okay.
The nurse asked did I have an appointment and I said no. She

told him, "Toi Culpepper is here." and even though he was with a patient, he immediately came out and was happy to see me. He said, "I will never forget you, your case will go down in history." Whoever is reading this, please know that God is real and Heaven is definitely real. I would like for people to know, whether you call it paradise, the after-life or Heaven, it does exist, so do angels and if you don't believe anything else, please believe, that God is real and no matter what you're going through, He hasn't forgotten you.

Everything you can imagine is real.

-Pablo Picasso

AMAZING TESTIMONY
by:
E. RANDALL
Retired

LITTLE ANGEL

I was born premature with a Rheumatic heart and two of my fingers were webbed together. The doctors had to cut and separate my fingers and then they grafted skin from my abdomen and placed it between them. During my elementary school years, my doctor informed me not to take gym class or swimming and he wrote a note to my teacher stating that I could not participate in these activities. He also informed me to never marry, have children or play a wind instrument. He said, "It will be too much for your heart to take." I tore the doctors notes up and decided to be determined to do the things in life I wanted to do. I felt like God would take care of me or He would take me young.

I was not only born with a webbed finger but I was fed through an eyedropper. My mother would take me back and forth to the hospital. I was six when I entered La Rabida Hospital, and while there, apparently, I took a turn for the worse. They thought I was dying so my mother called our pastor Rev. Johnson who had the gift of healing from God and laid hands on many people who were healed of various illnesses.

The first time my mother took me to see Rev. Johnson she told my mother, "You don't have enough faith to believe that God will heal your daughter and she's too young to have faith herself. Go back home, read your Bible and pray for faith to believe and know that God is a Healer, then you can bring her back."

When Rev. Johnson arrived at the hospital, I had the 'death rattle'. She picked me up and put me on her lap and began to pray. I remember vividly, an angel that was very pretty came and picked me up and the next thing I knew, we were flying

73

like a bird through bright blue and beautiful light. I looked down and saw there was bright white sparkling sand that I've never seen in life before.

There were two strips of beautiful blue water like this, each separated by this dazzling sand. It looked as if this phenomenal pattern was going on forever into the horizon. Then the angel put me down on the middle strips of sand and as I looked up I saw other angels carrying people in their arms going across to the other side of the blue water.

I asked my angel, "Why can't I go all the way across, why can't I go across?" I was the only one on the strip of sand. My angel said, "You're not going across this time." I started to hear someone calling my name way off in the distance. Later, I was told, it was Rev.

Johnson calling my name. As her voice got louder and closer, I came out of it and I was on her lap. I don't recall ever seeing wings on the angels and I never had an interest in angels prior to that as a child.

To this day, everything that the doctors said I couldn't do because of my heart, I have done. I took gym, I swam, I played the clarinet, and I got married and had two beautiful daughters who lived without any complications.

What this story conveyed to me, as a Christian, we often wonder, *are we going to make it in*? I often pray I'm worthy," but He let's me know that I am worthy through the life and death of Jesus Christ and because He loved me so much to die for my sins, I love him back and I am saved. I know I'll see that angel again and I will fly to the other side of that beautiful blue water in God's time.

AMAZING TESTIMONY
by:
JOHN GRIFFIN
Retired Chicago Police Officer/Detective

DISAPPEARING WALL

My legal name is John, but my family wanted me to be named Cornell. When I was three years old on the farm in Missouri with my grandparents, who I lived with for over a year, I developed measles and pneumonia at the same time. My grandmother who lived to be 101 years old, born April 23, 1893 and died April 23, 1994, had thirteen kids and she raised twenty-six kids.

She gave birth to my mother one day and was in the cotton fields picking cotton the next day. My biological grandfather was Mexican, Joe Montenia, but she married someone else. His name was Poppa Macintosh, a Native American, who I took a picture with on my third birthday, the same day he gave me a pet pony. Within weeks of my birthday I had a Near Death Experience.

I got the measles first which a lot of people don't know, if not treated, since it is a disease of your respiratory system, it will turn into pneumonia. Poppa rushed me to the nearest hospital. When we got to the hospital the doctors wouldn't treat me in Lilbourn, Missouri because I was Black.

My family had to bring me back to Chicago so I could be seen at the hospital. Poppa was holding me like a baby and I was looking up at the sky. It was a summer night when we got to the corner of King Drive and I believe I passed out. I was waking up from being unconscious and I heard the doctor tell my dad that I was in critical condition and wouldn't make it overnight. I was three and didn't know what critical meant, but I knew it was bad news.

That night in the hospital room, I woke up, looked at the wall and it literally disappeared. I didn't see a shadow or any more bed rails that had been there earlier to protect me. All I

saw was a yellow light. I sat up and went into that light and talked to my guardian angel, which was a woman with a very soft and familiar voice. She called me Cornell. I knew instinctively that at that moment I had a choice to go further into that light or come back and stay in that hospital room and with my family; I chose to stay.

I am glad I came back and grew up to be a police officer. I realized I picked the right profession where I could help many people. I recall one day after joining the police force, I got a call for an older lady who lived in a ranch house, and when I knocked on the door, no one answered. I went to the back door and it was open. I saw a woman sitting in a chair. She said, "Officer, I've been sitting here for three days praying for an angel to come." I said, "Baby, I don't claim to be an angel, but I'm here for you." I have countless stories of helping others through my years as a Police Officer and I am glad that I was given the opportunity to stay here on this earth at the age of three to fulfill that purpose.

It is never too late to be what you might have been.

-George Eliot

FEATURED AMAZING TESTIMONY

Just in case you didn't read my INTRODUCTION, I mentioned how many years ago, God gave me an idea. Yes, God. He spoke it into my heart and my spirit to write a book filled with real life testimonies of people from all walks of life to inspire people from all walks of life. I started, then stopped, then started and stopped again. I tried the idea of making videos of peoples' stories and procrastinated after shooting one day. I sat thinking to myself, years later, "Wow, I've wasted so much time."

I could have had several volumes of this book done by now. I could have collected thousands of stories from people including my own and shared them with the world, blessing, touching and inspiring others. I encourage you, as you continue to read this book, to be inspired to do the opposite of what I did and don't waste another minute on that idea that has been planted deep inside you. Use every talent, gift and anointing that God has given you and remember that procrastination is not an option.

It is a blessing to share this next story with you from someone who definitely does not waste one moment of his time on this earth.

<u>MEETING A MIRACLE:</u>

My husband introduced me to Daryl Vinson and his wife Margo during our dating years. I have come to love The Vinson's and their children.

I chose to feature Daryl in AMAZING TESTIMONIES because his story is incredible and his faith is tremendously inspirational. He and Margo have been through a lot, both on the operating table multiple times and both having experienced miracles that the doctor's just could not explain. In the future, I will share Margo's story as well but for now we will take a journey into the unbelievable experience of Mr. Daryl Vinson who has overcome more than most would have the strength to endure. To God Be the Glory.

AMAZING TESTIMONY
by:
DARYL VINSON
Entertainment and Business Executive
Daryl.Vinson@live.com

HEAVENLY HEART TRANSPLANT

I was thirty-eight years old when I passed out driving one day. I was headed to church one morning and I felt a little ill. I was living in Hollywood Hills and while I was coming down one of the hills toward an intersection, it felt like someone was turning me off slowly as if I was a dimmer on a light. I was fully awake, saying, "What's happening? It feels like I'm being turned off."

As I was saying that out loud as I slumped over the armrest and passed out, but the car was still moving. When I came to, it frightened me because I knew I had gone through at least two intersections. I'm a former serviceman so much doesn't scare me, but this did. When I woke up and became coherent of my surroundings, I regained control of the steering wheel. Something prompted me to look to the left and there was a hospital.

I went inside and spoke to the receptionist and she asked me for my insurance card. As I was giving it to her, things got blurry and I passed out again.

I was admitted into the hospital for approximately four days. The doctors couldn't figure out what was wrong with me. I spoke with my fiancée at the time (now my wife, Margo) over the phone and I told her what happened and that it had something to do with my heart, but they couldn't confirm it. She said, "Have you ever seen the movie about *John Q*? It's about a boy who had a heart condition and needed a heart transplant and the father, played by Denzel Washington, couldn't afford it so the father took an employee hostage to operate on Denzel, take his heart and give it to his son."

I said, "Well, that's not me," and I got a little irritated that she was asking me all these questions about a movie that I didn't want to talk about. Just as I said that, I happened to look up and see that very movie on the television in my hospital room. The opening credits suddenly appeared on television.

I said, "Margo, guess what just came on the television?" She said, "John Q."

I said, "Yes, John Q."

She said, "You're supposed to watch that movie."

I got off the phone with her and watched the movie. I never watched a film so intensely. I didn't even get up to go to the bathroom. I even watched every commercial just as intensely. I wept and cried as I watched a father willing to sacrifice his life for his son. I thought of my own son who was only seven months old at the time.

I was released from the hospital with a clean bill of health, or so I thought. I was sleeping a lot, at work and at home. One day at work, I wasn't feeling well. I went home early and asked my secretary to bring my work to my new place, which was a block from the school where I worked. I decided to move after the incident in the car so I wouldn't have far to travel. I asked her to bring me some water and when she arrived, I suddenly felt very ill. Every time I would lie down it felt like someone was holding me under water. I finally sat up and sweated all night long.

At 6:00 a.m., I woke up, looked over and sitting on my couch was my secretary. I said, "What are you doing here?"

She said, "Mr. Vinson, I have been here all night praying for you. You've been very sick all night."

Margo called and I told her what happened, including the part about my secretary. She encouraged me to call Don Ross, who was my business partner and mentor. He was a former executive for a major film studio and I trusted him like a father figure. I called Don and he immediately came and got me. He said, "I need to take you to a doctor who can help you. His name is Darryl Houston and he has an incredible gift for medicine and I know he can help you."

Once we arrived at Dr. Houston's office, I was surprised to see he was an African-American doctor with the same name as me. He listened to my heart and to my lungs, and stared at me. I asked him, "What's wrong? What's going on?"

He sat down and stared at me, and started to write something down. He asked me if I had any relatives. I said, "My fiancée is out of town and Don is the only one here."

He said, "Don is the closest person here to you? Do you have any children? Where's your mother? What are their numbers?" He wrote their numbers down.

"Why are you asking me all of this?"

He turned and looked at me. "Mr. Vinson, I have very bad news for you. You are in stage 4 heart failure and you have forty-eight hours to live."

I said, "You have me confused with another patient. I was just running on the football field days ago, doing four hundred sit-ups. You have got me confused."

He said, "I wish I did."

He called Margo, told her the news and requested that if she wanted to see me alive, she should get to Los Angeles immediately and bring my son. He called my mother and told her the same thing. I went to the window and stared out of it, trying to figure out what was going on and what was wrong with me.

Across the street was the very hospital where I would soon be fighting for my life.

He said, "I need to admit you to the hospital." I refused, saying, "No, I'm in great shape."

He said, "Fine, I will give you one week."

The very next day, he put me in a clinic for treatment and my heart began to fail there. I knew my life was hanging in the balance. I asked Don to take me to the bank to pull out the money to give to him so he could go buy Margo and my son a ticket to get to Los Angeles.

We drove from Los Angeles to Compton to the bank. We got to the bank and I felt okay. As soon as we left out of the bank, I felt a sense of peace and relief, knowing that Margo and my son were coming to Los Angeles. The minute we left the bank, I collapsed in the parking lot. Several firefighters, who happened to be in the bank, came over to help me. They wanted to take me to a local hospital. Don knew I had to get back to Dr. Houston who diagnosed me. I said, "Just help me get to the car."

The minute I got in the car, I started to vomit. He started and stopped the car multiple times so I could vomit. Don had a vintage 1980 Mercedes-Benz. It was a four-door with the phone in the middle console. It was in immaculate condition because he never drove it. Being a studio executive, a car would always pick him up so he didn't drive that car as often. It only had 24,000 miles on it.

He continued to pull over to the side of the road all the way to the freeway, while I continued to vomit. Once we got to the freeway, I reclined the seat. The minute we got on the 105 Freeway, I felt a peace come over me. Later, he would tell me that he drove 110 miles per hour in that car. He said he didn't even know the car could go that fast. As I was looking up, the sun was beaming on me and it was literally getting closer and closer to me. I felt the warmth of the sun all over my body; it seemed like it was coming through the windshield.

All I wanted to do was sleep. I said, "Don, let me take a nap." He was on the speakerphone with Dr. Houston, who could hear me.

"You must keep him awake, Don," Dr. Houston said, "because he is dying."

Later, Don told me that he was slapping and punching me to keep me awake. He said, "I beat the crap out of you and you didn't even know it. I hit you so hard and you just kept talking about how warm the sun felt." I didn't feel a thing.

Don was hoping the police didn't get behind him. He said, "I was not going to stop," and as fast as he was going, the police probably wouldn't have caught him anyway. He floored it and he doesn't remember how he got to the hospital, but all he knew was that he was there. He told me, "I don't remember stopping at the light or even knowing what exit I came off of." Don pulled up to the ER, jumped out, and took me to the receptionist window. The receptionist was asking me questions, but she sounded like the lady from *Charlie Brown*.

I asked Don, "Why does she sound like *Charlie Brown*? Wah wah wahh wahh."

She came around the desk, looked at me, and got me on a gurney. I passed out and when I woke up, Dr. Houston was standing over me.

"Daryl it doesn't look good," Dr. Houston said. "We have to get you to Cedars Sinai Medical Center as soon as possible." They admitted me at Cedars and it took them three days to get me stable.

On the third day, Dr. Houston said, "We have a bed for you," referring to Cedars Sinai.

Years later, he told me, "It was a miracle from God that we got you in Cedars." He had made a special call to a friend of his, who wasn't supposed to be on duty, but he stayed at work, tired; however, he felt like he was supposed to be there. I never met this young man, but Dr. Houston said the young man was instrumental in getting me into the clinic by contacting the other doctors directly.

An ambulance came to transport me and they immediately put me into ICU critical care. Once there, it was the most beautiful hospital I had ever seen. It looked like something out of *Star Wars*. Everything was round and shaped like a horseshoe and there were flat screen televisions everywhere. Everything was made of glass so you could look out of each room and see the nurse's station.

This was the VIP section, and I later found out the late Merv Griffin was two beds down and the late actress Isabel Sanford was right across from me. Nurses were clipping my toenails and giving me baths. One of the nurses asked me, "Are you Snoop Dogg?" People were trying to figure out who I was.

I found out from both of my doctors, one who had white hair and powerful hands and another who looked like Brad Pitt, that I was at the end stage of heart failure and the only chance of survival for me was going to be an immediate heart transplant.

They said, "Our job now is to keep you alive and to give you a heart transplant." They introduced me to a lady named Ellen who was my case social worker. She talked with me about having a Will made because I was possibly going to die. She also talked to me about the different hearts I could get from either prisoners, criminals, John Does, etc. She said, "But because you're at Cedars, you are going to get the best heart out there. We only look for A-list organs, but if we don't find one, are you open to taking whatever comes through?" I was okay with it and then a lady came in wearing a suit, holding a pen and paper in hand and the doctors were also behind her.

I said, "Oh, it's time to pay the piper."

The lady bluntly said, without any exchange of pleasantries, "How do you plan on paying for this?"

I said, "Just pass me my wallet."

Everyone found it amusing except for her. I meant it because I felt like, *I ain't scared of you*. They passed me my wallet.

"I've got a VA card. You guys take VA?" She replied, "No."

I innocently asked if they accepted debit as a form of payment. She looked at me as if I was being sarcastic.

She then said, "Mr. Vinson, just for you being here will be $180,000."

I mentioned that I had an annuity, but she proceeded to tell me, "Mr. Vinson, this is very serious; this could cost you $8 to $10 million."

I said, "Let's see." I pulled out my Blue Cross Blue Shield with an executive plan.

She said, "They still may turn you down."

The doctor said, "Let me see that. I know the president of Blue Cross. He's my neighbor. I will call him personally and talk to him about you so we can get this all resolved." He then advised "The likelihood of them approving this is very slim, but we will give it a shot."

I laid back and prayed, Lord, all of this is in Your hands. All of it belongs to You. I need You to help me because there's nothing I can do. A peace came over me and I said, "I'm not gonna worry about it. I'm just going to watch TV."

I turned on TBN. Benny Hinn was on and he prophesied. He began to speak... "There is a young man lying in a cardiac unit right now and God says to tell you, "It's going to be all right. He's going to heal your heart and everything will be okay."

This was at 7 a.m., and at close to 11:30 a.m., the surgeon came in and said, "Mr. Vinson, I've got some news for you and I've never seen this before. Blue Cross is not only approving you for a heart transplant, but they will put $10 million in your account." He continued, "I didn't have to call my friend. They approved this in two hours. No one called me, nor asked me questions; it just came in fully approved in your name under your account. All you should do is sign. Somebody likes you because I didn't have to call anyone."

I signed the Blue Cross Blue Shield insurance payment for $10 million. God used that money to fight for me. The hospital hired twenty-five doctors and twice as many nurses for my case. It was like my own medical operation going on.

After the Insurance approval, I received a call from a man named Pastor Arlan Sanchez whom I had never met. Apparently, he talked to Margo's girlfriend, Tanya, who was a member of Pastor Sanchez's church, The Covenant. Tanya told him about my circumstances. I remembered seeing her at the

hospital, standing outside my door, praying and worshipping. The doctors were saying that I might not make it because my prognosis was very grim and my heart was failing at twenty-five percent.

The doctors couldn't understand why the other organs in my body weren't failing. My heart would drop to two percent per day until it was down to less than five percent. I received a call from Pastor Sanchez before noon. "Daryl Vinson, this is Arlan Sanchez. They say I'm supposed to know you, but I don't remember you. This I do know, that you are a man of faith. The Lord says don't take the pacemaker. Whatever you do, don't take the pacemaker. I hope to see you soon. God, bless you." I hung up the phone and thought, *Okay, that was a strange phone call.*

I've been around the prophetic my whole life so I understand it and I didn't throw the message away, but I didn't think anything else about it. The next day at 4:00 a.m., my nurses got me up to bathe me. The doctors came by at 6:00 a.m. with a few more doctors. One had flaming red hair like Opie from *The Andy Griffith Show*.

One of them said, "Daryl we want to talk to you about giving you a pacemaker."

I had to sit up in the bed for that news. They told me how this would save my life. In case my heart stopped, there would be something in place to jumpstart it.

I was given the doctor's credentials and told to prep for surgery that same day to get the pacemaker. At that moment, I heard the Word of the Lord ringing in my ear saying, *Don't take the pacemaker.* I was lying there, looking at some of the best doctors with all these credentials talking to me. I thought about Pastor Sanchez and said to myself, *He doesn't have a PhD; he's not an MD.* The Holy Spirit spoke to me and said, *Whose report will you believe, the report of man or my report?*

I looked at them as they finished speaking, and I said, "Dr. Gaines, I'm not going to take the pacemaker."

Everyone was in shock.

He looked at me and squinted, "What did you say?"

"I'm not taking the pacemaker."

He asked again, "What did you say?" "I said, I'm not taking the pacemaker."

He firmly said, "How dare you say that to me? I'm trying to save your life! You've got one foot in the grave and another on a banana peel."

I calmly stated, "My life isn't yours to save."

He then went forward in saying, "Well, you might as well sign your own death certificate because you're going to die."

"If I die, so be it, it's not because the hand of God is too short that He could not save me. It's because it's my time to go and I will not accept a pacemaker."

He took his pad, slammed it on the foot of my bed, and stormed out of my room. The other doctors asked me if I was okay.

Two days later, they were running more tests on me and prepping me to go in for surgery to look at my heart. One of the nurses came running in the room, sliding in on one foot. She said, "Mr. Vinson, we've got to talk to you." She was mumbling and saying inaudible things, running out of the room and back in awkwardly.

The doctor who looked like Brad Pitt came into my room and said, "I have to apologize to you. As we were looking at your chart, something spoke to me and told me to send your chart with the recent blood work over to an older doctor at UCLA." This doctor told him if they cut me open, I would die on the operating table. All the people had signed off on this chart, but this doctor from UCLA said, "He is allergic to Heparin."

They would have had to give me Heparin to insert the pacemaker. The doctor continued, "I apologize to you because if you had accepted the pacemaker, we would have flooded your system with Heparin and you would have been dead on the table. Now we must go back to the drawing board and start over. Heparin is what we use to keep the blood flowing for these types of surgeries. That's the only drug that is used in the world."

They kept me there for several days, trying to figure out how they could save my life. They shipped a doctor to Cedars and my case was the first case he decided to take at the hospital. He told them that he had done some experimental work on patients with leeches and he knew a doctor in the northern hemisphere who used leeches. He also told me the doctors unknowingly were going to send me home to die. He informed me that he spoke five languages fluently and he had

done surgeries using leeches from Africa. He confidently let me know he was one of two doctors in the entire world that had practiced using leeches. He lastly, sympathetically said, "Something told me I was supposed to come to Los Angeles, even though my wife and I had decided not to come, and when I got here, they gave me your case."

After listening, I then asked, "What is the success rate with these leeches?"

He said, "Everyone has died."

My next question was, "What if I survive?"

He happily said, "If you survive, we would make history and we would save the lives of hundreds of thousands of people because you are not the only one allergic to Heparin."

My response was, "Well, doc, let's make history."

I reached out my hand to shake his and he busted out laughing and said, "You know what? Something tells me you are going to survive." He pulled out a huge needle from his pocket and said, "This is a sedative that I give to people when I tell them they are going to die because they usually break down. But, I have a feeling you are going to make it."

There was a woman in one of the rooms who had children and she lost it when they gave her the news that she would die. She could have used that sedative at one point, but the nurses told her to talk to me and she would be encouraged because I was way worse off than she was. I talked to her and ministered to her about God and she ended up getting better and eventually going home.

In my state, with less than twenty-five percent of my heart, I should have been on life support. The doctors would look at me in awe because I was still walking around and talking. They couldn't fathom that I was hanging out in the cafeteria, eating dinner with friends and family.

This was when they sent for the leeches. The doctors were shipping in live leeches from Africa to Los Angeles. After the leeches arrived, they began the process and subtracted the saliva from certain leeches that helped the doctors create an organic blood thinner for me that does what the Heparin would have done. They fired Dr. Gaines from my case because of his behavior and restricted him from coming to see me. Although restricted to do so, he did come by at 3:00 a.m. one morning and he apologized to me with great humility.

He said, "I am so sorry."

I told him that I appreciated him for wanting to save my life and for having such passion about wanting me to live. So many supernatural things happened in that hospital during the time I was there. After the leeches, there was an incident where everyone in the ward started to die.

As I mentioned earlier, the ward was set up in an octagon horseshoe with glass windows. The nurse's station was positioned in the middle. You could pull your curtain back, look out, and see everything. The walls could retract and immediately turn into a surgical room. I started to hear "Code blue! Code blue!" Suddenly, patients all over the ward began to scream out. The woman in the room next to me had been in a coma since the time I was admitted several weeks earlier and she woke up suddenly screaming bloody murder. She was fighting the doctors and nurses and trying to run. She started fighting things in the air that no one else could see, saying, "Get away from me! I'm not going!" She was terrified of what she saw. She was speaking in English and in her native Chinese language.

They brought a priest to read her last rights. He was never able to finish the rights. She died kicking and screaming as if she was being tormented. It was like spirits came to get her and she was being dragged to hell. I prayed, worshipped, and turned on my gospel music. All day, screaming was going on and I listened to a lot of Fred Hammond's worship music. I asked a nurse, "What is my room number?"

"Why?" she asked.

"Because if y'all calling code blue, I want to know if it's me."

That evening, that same nurse came into my room and again I asked what's going on. She didn't want to tell me, so I emphatically said, "What's going on?"

She said, "I'm not supposed to tell you this, but Dr. Czer wants to move you off the floor now." She urgently grabbed my things, made some calls and I demanded she tell me what was happening. She continued, "Dr. Czer said a spirit of death is sweeping through the ward and you and one other person are the only ones left alive." They covered me up, moved me out into a hidden room in the hospital, and set up an ICU ward specifically for me. As they were taking me out, I heard code blue for the other surviving patient and then he died.

Dr. Czer told me later, "Daryl, I've seen it before. It is the spirit of death and everyone in the other ward and in your ward died except for you." They hid me and I felt like Moses because when they came to kill all the young men in Egypt, they hid Moses. During the time of Moses, the spirit of death swept through Egypt, but those who had the blood of the Lamb, which represents Jesus, were saved.

I can't tell you where it was, but the doctor said, "They have to have a rabbi come, and clean the ward spiritually with prayer before any other patients can go back into that ward."

God put doctors and nurses around me that were spiritual and sensitive. When I went into surgery, I died on that table. When I woke up, darkness covered me like a heavy mink blanket and there was so much peace. Over my right shoulder, a hand came and it was like it had stars in it. A presence in my right ear said, "Wake up!

Wake up!" I was in surgery.

I looked around and said, "Well, this can't be Heaven. I remember that nurse and I remember him."

The nurse looked down in my face and said, "Dr. Czer, I think Mr. Vinson is awake." He said, "What?"

"I think Mr. Vinson is awake."

He and all the nurses looked down into my face and he said, "Mr. Vinson, if you can hear me, give me a sign that you can hear me." I gave a thumbs-up like Fonzie from Happy Days.

The nurse said, "Knock him out! Knock him out now!"

The doctors told me later, "We put you under so deep there is no way you could wake up. You were supposed to be in a drug-induced coma for seventy-two hours." They told Margo and Don, "If we don't call you in seventy-two hours, he didn't make it."

After surgery, I woke up again out of the coma in post-op. My assigned nurse was a Hispanic guy named Henry who was a man of God. Twelve hours later when I woke up, I looked at Henry and said, "Henry, you gotta call my fiancée now. I need to speak to my fiancée!"

He made the call. Fear gripped her and Don when the call came in because the caller ID showed it was the hospital. Don answered the phone.

"Don, this is Daryl. Daryl?"

"Yeah, I'm calling from the other side." I didn't know I had scared them so bad. Margo was frozen; she couldn't answer the phone.

The surgery was successful and I am blessed to have the heart of a young thirty-year-old Caucasian man named Mark. I just spoke to his Mom the other day. When the heart came in, they said, "We have never had a match so perfect. The only difference between the two of you is race. The man was brain dead and he had told his mom he wanted to donate his organs." Mark was out on his four-wheeler when he had fallen off and as he was lying in the yard, he had a brain aneurism.

Mark's mom was at the hospital, sitting there with her girlfriend, when the people came and asked for his organs. She couldn't believe it, she was thinking, *How can you ask me this and he's not even dead?* His friends had set up a makeshift memorial area down in the waiting room on the table. She looked up and saw Jesus Christ walk into the room. This woman was not a Christian at the time. She said to her friend, "Do you see what I see? That's Jesus." Her friend said, "Yes." He stood before them, a peace came over her, and He looked over at the memorial and then smiled at her. Something said to her, *Give them the heart it will be okay.* Jesus turned and walked straight through the hospital entrance door.

A lady came to her and said, "Would you let us have his heart?"

She said, "Yes," and a peace came over her. She saw limousines roll up and a helicopter land.

The doctor walked up to her and said, "Thank you so much." No one had thanked her, but him. She watched him get into one of the limousines and then pull off. His license plate read: Top Dog. While people walked past her and took her son's body apart, my doctor was the only one who thanked her.

They looked outside and under the tree to see Jesus sitting there and smiling. Her encounter reminded me of a dream I had years ago about my own death. I was in heaven sitting under a tree and Jesus was walking in a garden. He came to me and said, "My son, what is troubling you?"

I responded, "I didn't get a chance to fulfill my purpose on earth." Jesus said, "Go back and finish what you've started."

After Mark's mom told me what happened and how she and her friend saw Jesus, I knew at that moment that Jesus sitting

under the tree represented him taking my place so I could fulfill my purpose.

God is a healer. When the doctor took my heart out and replaced it with Mark's, he told me later that my heart was hard as rock, it was literally dead. In Ezekiel 36:26 it says, *I will give you a new heart and put a new spirit in you; I will remove from you your heart of stone and give you a heart of flesh*. If we would believe and trust God, there is nothing impossible with God. With man, it is impossible, but with God, all things are possible. I had a dead heart and I am still alive. He will show Himself to be strong. I just know it.

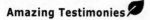

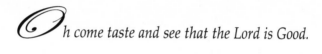

Oh come taste and see that the Lord is Good.

SCRIPTURES ON NEAR DEATH
EXPERIENCES

---

³² When Elisha reached the house, there was the boy lying dead on his couch. ³³ He went in, shut the door on the two of them and prayed to the Lord. ³⁴ Then he got on the bed and lay on the boy, mouth to mouth, eyes to eyes, hands to hands. As he stretched himself out on him, the boy's body grew warm. ³⁵ Elisha turned away and walked back and forth in the room and then got on the bed and stretched out on him once more. The boy sneezed seven times and opened his eyes.
2 Kings 4:32-35

⁴⁰ Then Jesus said, "Did I not tell you that if you believe, you will see the glory of God?" ⁴¹ So they took away the stone. Then Jesus looked up and said, "Father, I thank you that you have heard me. ⁴² I knew that you always hear me, but I said this for the benefit of the people standing here, that they may believe that you sent me." ⁴³ When he had said this, Jesus called in a loud voice, "Lazarus, come out!" ⁴⁴ The dead man came out, his hands and feet wrapped with strips of linen, and a cloth around his face. Jesus said to them,
"Take off the grave clothes and let him go."
John 11: 40-44

⁴⁹ While Jesus was still speaking, someone came from the house of Jairus, the synagogue leader. "Your daughter is dead," he said. "Don't bother the teacher anymore." ⁵⁰ Hearing this, Jesus said to Jairus, "Don't be afraid; just believe, and she will be healed." ⁵¹ When he arrived at the house of Jairus, he did not let anyone go in with him except Peter, John and James, and the child's father and mother. ⁵² Meanwhile, all the people were wailing and mourning for her. "Stop wailing," Jesus said. "She is not dead but asleep." ⁵³ They laughed at him, knowing that she was dead. ⁵⁴ But he took her by the hand and said, "My child, get up!" ⁵⁵ Her spirit returned, and at once she stood up. Then Jesus told them to give her something to eat. ⁵⁶ Her parents were astonished, but he ordered them not to tell anyone what

had happened.
Luke 8:49-56

50 And when Jesus had cried out again in a loud voice, he gave up his spirit. 51 At that moment the curtain of the temple was torn in two from top to bottom. The earth shook, the rocks split 52 and the tombs broke open. The bodies of many holy people who had died were raised to life. 53 They came out of the tombs after Jesus' resurrection and went into the holy city and appeared to many people.
Matthew 27:50-53

Why Are You Weeping? God Is Not Dead.

CHAPTER 5

VICTIM TO VICTOR

I don't like the word "Victim," but when I look back on my life since childhood, so many situations I've experienced that fall under that category come to mind.

It seemed as if my classmates bullied me for years. If they weren't beating my sister Tasha and me up after school just because we had long hair, they were threatening me in the bathroom stalls or cutting my school blouse with scissors trying desperately to cut my hair or cornering me in the hallway telling me what they were going to do to me later. I eventually learned how to fight back and defend myself because I got sick of getting beat up.

To make matters worse, I used to be really skinny. My older cousin, Clara Flewellen, who the entire church endearingly referred to as "Mama Flew", called me "Bones". I would run in another direction when I saw her coming to shield myself from the embarrassment of hearing that horrible nickname which gave the other children ammunition to make fun of me. "Bones! Come here Bones!" Mama Flew would yell down Antioch Missionary Baptist Church corridors.

Then there was the time I woke up in second grade to a dark ring around my mouth that eventually started to crack, bleed, and puss. It wasn't the prettiest thing and I endured being called "The Monster" by the majority of my fellow students in Altgeld Gardens, Our Lady of The Gardens grammar school. I dreaded going outside for recess every day because I knew what was waiting for me so I would lag behind on purpose. The minute I walked through the door the playground would erupt into screams as various kids yelled, "Here comes the monster! Run, here comes the monster!"

Every day for months, I would cry until one day I decided, "If you can't beat 'em, join 'em." I walked outside, heard the familiar monster name and then I put both my hands up like claws and growled like a real monster, "Raah, I'm gonna get cha!" The kids screamed and ran from me and I chased them all over the playground. I figured somebody was going to play with me one way or another. Kids-they can be so mean. It was that moment that I decided I would love on and protect every person who was mistreated because I didn't want anyone to experience the pain I went through daily.

The funny thing is I never saw myself as a victim during the circumstances. However, through the years as people would hear my story or stories, they were the ones to label me a victim.

After a break up once, my ex fiancé looked at me and very arrogantly and non–compassionately asked me, "Are you feeling like a victim Trish?" The word hadn't entered my mind, but if you weighed his treatment of me, then yes, I could have been a victim, but I did not claim that title. I simply walked away from him and moved forward in my life. I had already experienced enough pain from a past relationship, which had to be the worst relationship I ever had. I have often wondered how many of my relationship experiences stem from the root of my childhood.

When I was six years old, it seemed like my entire family was over my grandmother's house for a big party and I was being babysat by two twin sister's upstairs. I remember their cream- colored skin, long brown hair, keen noses, and large breasts. Their breasts stood out the most because they forced me to touch them and they made me play "Baby" while they tried to breast feed me. These young ladies molested me in my own bedroom while my mother and father, grandparents, aunts and uncles were downstairs.

Everyone who could have protected me were right there, downstairs underneath me, laughing and eating and having a good time, oblivious to the activities going on above them. My babysitters warned me not to tell anyone what they had done. I was so respectful of older people I thought I had to do what these two teenagers told me to do; yet as young as I was, in my spirit I knew something was wrong about what took place in my room.

It would be thirty plus years later before I even told someone that story and a few months after that when I would forgive the twin sisters in my heart for what they did. I was a victim of molestation and throughout the years I would learn of other people's experiences and how much worse their situations were. I would also learn about the spiritually wicked

door that is open because of these occurrences and how it can make you act out on your own peers, but I would come to understand that every door opened can also be closed through deliverance.

I grew up in a loving environment. For the first ten years of my life, I watched my mother and father love on each other. They were affectionate with one another and I only heard them argue one time, which was right before their shocking divorce.

I remember the day my mother broke the news to me about my parent's divorce. I jumped up from the kitchen table, ran into the bathroom, and cried my eyes out. I heard my mother walking swiftly in the bathroom behind me saying, "How could you do this to me?" Words my ten-year old mind could not comprehend at the time, but years later would realize more when I learned that Dad had suddenly been brainwashed into believing in Polygamy and wanted my mother to comply with his unethical desires at the time.

Mom refused to have my sister and I grow up in a household where we would witness our father being affectionate with not just our mother, but other women who would have a hand in raising us as well. Fifteen years of marriage with two children down the drain because of a fantasy and fleshly desires, but either way, it would have affected me just as the incident with the sisters had affected me.

The divorce put so much distance between my father and me to the point that I got used to him missing my birthdays or recitals or father-daughter dances at school and then he moved to California which meant huge gaps of time before I would talk to him or let alone see him. I was truly a Daddy's girl and I missed my father so much, but to me, it didn't seem like he cared anymore. I was silently searching for a replacement. I thank God that, years later I forgave him and we began healing our relationship in my late twenties. He's grown to be a wonderful man.

During my dating years, I didn't have any one specific type of guy that I liked so I dated all different types. However, I was searching for something, but I wasn't quite sure what or who. Academically, I was doing great in College and socially the same.

I had just won the Miss Black Chicago pageant, I had released a song that was getting airplay, I had been doing print work for Ebony and Jet magazines, and I had just pledged my sorority, Delta Sigma Theta Sorority, Inc.. I was also active in

96

my church and I was working in the Philosophy and the Math Department at the University where I was attending school full time.

My life seemed amazing and I was very content until I met the guy I thought was my 'dream come true' and that he would fill that void that I needed to be filled. He was sweet, attentive, and affectionate the way my father was with my mom before the divorce. He always said the right things and was Mr. Handy Man, there to fix everything even in my mom's house.

The whole family met him and thought he was the nicest young man I had dated yet. I had everyone's approval. One day, he came over to my place and asked me to move to another city two hours away from my friends and family. He promised me that if I took off my last year from school and helped him with his dream of opening a restaurant and dance club, he would give me twenty-thousand dollars to help toward me going back to school. That was an unrealistic goal that never manifested into reality. Even when he first said it, I didn't really count on it, but I was hopeful.

I only had a year left to finish school, but I was so far gone into this young man, I couldn't see straight. Against my mother's wishes, friend's advice and the Record Company threats, I "brilliantly" moved away to follow someone else's dream. Fred, the president of the record company said, "Trisha, you have a record that is being played and going from slow rotation to medium rotation at the radio stations in some cities and high rotation in a few others. We have an album to finish so don't go chasing some boy when you've got your whole life ahead of you."

I responded, "It's just two hours away. I can always drive back and forth to work on the album." The last words I would ever hear the president of the record company say to me were, "If you leave Chicago, I'm dropping you from the label like a hot potato." I left Chicago and he proved he meant every word; I have not spoken to him or seen him since.

My mother warned me about shacking up with my newfound love and begged me to finish school so I could have my degree to fall back on. My friends said, "How much do you really know about the brother?" I did what every hardheaded girl who thinks she's in love would do, I did it my way and my way would soon prove to be the wrong way.

I let my cousin Clay live in my apartment when I left. Clay had moved to America from Turkey, to get to know his dad, my

uncle Robby who met his mother while he was in the service. A few years later, after Clay being here, Uncle Robby died but I took Clay under my wing, helped teach him English and he lived with me. Then I was swept off my feet and changing my whole lifestyle for the sake of love. Clay was the only one who wasn't fond of my boyfriend. In fact, he had an instant disdain for him, it was almost as if he knew something I didn't. I remember the day I was packing to leave I experienced a supernatural sign that I wouldn't understand until years later.

As I put clothes into my suitcase, a very dark feeling of sadness came over me, almost like an instant depression and I began to cry hard and long and uncontrollably for no reason at all. At that moment, I didn't know that I was entering into what would be one of the most difficult times of my life from a mere decision. I had only been gone for a month when my mother called me with the news that Clay had been shot and killed while being robbed blocks away from my apartment in Hyde Park. He refused a blood transfusion in the ambulance because of his Muslim beliefs and he didn't make it through that night. My cousin, Clay's life became an exchange for a little bit of money in his wallet.

After Clay's funeral, I continued to live with my boyfriend and help him get his restaurant and dance club up and going. I was the waitress, bartender, cook, cleaning lady, cashier at the door, and sometimes the deejay when the deejay didn't show up and I did it all because I loved him. I was determined to be the team player and "Ride or Die" partner. Unfortunately, I would find out that his ex- girlfriend lived there and I was being used in every sense to get her back.

One day he invited her to come and work the door once we opened the restaurant's club doors. It was so disrespectful to me, but I didn't say a word. When she walked in, his friend's mouths dropped because they all knew he and I were together. She was a pretty, brown-skinned tall girl that walked with her head held high and an intense air of arrogance. She passed by as if to say, "Move heifer, the queen has arrived." I watched her saunter over to the cash register, take my boyfriend's instructions and within thirty minutes I saw her get angry with him and throw the money down because he kept checking on her and telling her what to do. She left as quickly as she came, so guess who had to work the door? Yep, yours truly. His hopes and failure to get her back may have been the catalyst for the negative treatment I would soon endure. It wasn't long before he began to say mean, derogatory things to me for no reason, which I would later come to understand was verbal abuse.

One day I was too skinny, the next not pretty enough, the next day I was told, "You would be nothing if it weren't for me." The interesting thing is that he was drawn to me because of who I was and the accomplishments I had before he entered my life.

Slowly, my self-esteem that I never had a problem with was being torn to pieces and then, if I questioned anything that seemed wrong, unethical or looked shady, I would see objects come flying past me and slamming into the walls or my pager smashed to pieces. The woman I am today would never stand for that, but since I had already lost a huge sense of self-worth back then and during all of this, found out I was pregnant, I stayed.

He asked me to marry him in spite of the abuse and all I could think about was the slap I received during an argument. That slap was so hard that my jaw clicked and made a popping sound every time I talked for about a month. I believe if the slap had been slightly harder, my jaw would have been dislocated. All I could think about were all the female patrons that seemed to be very familiar with him and the evidence of him cheating that he always denied. I remembered the shoe that flew past my pregnant stomach because I asked a simple question and the dent it left in the wall from hitting it so hard.

Then I thought about my mother being disgusted with me bringing a child into this world out of wedlock or the baby growing up not knowing his father. I was even delusional enough to think that there was a small possibility that this man would actually change once the baby got here and treat me better. I considered getting married and I started planning the wedding. Then I prayed.

One night, while he was gone doing God knows what, I sat on the floor of our apartment writing out our wedding list. I put the pen down, crossed my legs Indian style and I said this simple prayer, "Lord I am going to marry this man so that I don't bring my son into this world out of wedlock, but Father, if it is not your will that I marry him, please give me a sign. Amen."

Week's prior to this prayer, he hired a pretty young lady who was half German and half Black. I thought she was very sweet and I had no problem with her, but one day as I passed the walk-in cooler, I turned and saw the both of them inside

facing each other, smiling and he was singing, R. Kelly's song, "Bump and Grind" to her. She was blushing as he sang, *"My mind is telling me no, but my body is telling me yes."*

I quickly rushed to the restroom because earlier that week I had been sensing that something was going on between the two of them and when I questioned him about it he said, "Trisha, your insecurity is going to push me away. I don't want that B-----!" His mouth was saying one thing, but my intuition was telling me something else. I had never heard him call a woman out of her name like that, but I still didn't buy it.

After asking God to give me a sign the night I prayed, the very next morning I woke up to a voice in my right ear saying, *"Get up."* I opened my eyes and saw that no one else was in the room. *"Get up"* the voice said again. I was not afraid and instantly knew that this was an Angelic experience, however, it was very strange because I had never heard an Angel or the Holy Spirit speak to me audibly. In fact, back then I really didn't think it was possible. Oh, but oh, have I grown.

I was obedient and I got up, the voice then said, *"Get dressed."* I walked quietly into the bathroom, took a quick birdbath and got dressed not knowing what to expect next. Immediately after getting dressed, my next command came, *"Go to the club."* I went to my car, didn't turn the radio on, but I drove to the restaurant and proceeded to park outside of it. The voice said, *"No, park over there."* I instinctively turned my head to the left and saw a parking place in another area across the street where my car would not have been seen.

At this point I knew that God was trying to reveal something to me and I was bracing myself for whatever was about to happen. I got out of the car, walked up to the front door and the voice said, *"No, go through the back."* I had never gone up the back steps to get in, but the voice or Holy Spirit seemed to know more than me so I continued to obey. As I was walking up the back stairs, the spirit said, *"Be very quiet,"* so I tiptoed quietly up the stairs and when I reached the door at the top, I saw my boyfriend standing behind the bar with his back to me.

He was searching the front door prepared to hang up if he saw me come in. He was on the phone talking about me, telling this person who was apparently a female all kinds of lies, and embellishing about an argument we had the day before. I stood close behind him and he didn't feel my presence for a while. It seemed as if God was giving me enough time to hear what I needed to hear and then suddenly he turned around, saw me, and nearly jumped out of his skin.

"Who are you talking to?" I asked firmly. He quickly said goodbye to the person and abruptly hung up the phone. I promptly picked it up and tried to dial *69 which would dial the number back right away, but he pushed the buttons on the phone before I hit the number nine.

"Who were you talking to?" I asked again.

"That was my boy in Chicago, he called and asked me how we were doing, and I told him about our argument earlier and…" The Holy Spirit said in my right ear as he continued to elaborate, *"He's lying."*

I looked him dead in his eyes and I said, "You're lying." He looked at me as if he knew without a doubt that I knew he was lying.

I then took matters in my own hands and pretended to be emotional and plead with him to tell me the truth, promising not to get upset. "Please just tell me who you were talking to, I need to know, I promise I won't get mad." He finally succumbed and said the young lady's name that I saw in the cooler goo-goo eyeing him and I lost it.

"I knew it! I knew something was going on between you two! How could you do this to me?"

I didn't realize at the time that we had a patron inside eating lunch so he grabbed my arm and rushed me to the bathroom where we had it out. I was so caught up in my emotions that the Holy Spirit had backed up from me at this point until I calmed down and stopped operating in my "flesh." In the women's room, our rage continued as he told me how he didn't like her, or want her and that she was weird. He told me I was being stupid because nothing happened between them. I decided to leave the club and go home. He said, "Good." I ran down the back stairs crying and once again I heard the voice say, *"Stop, go back."*

I was obedient and unbeknownst to him I went back into the ladies' room, dried my tears, and calmed down. Little did I know that he had gotten back on the phone with her and told her to come to the club. *"Leave the bathroom."* The voice said. I was heading back down the backstairs when I heard, *"Go through the kitchen."* As I went through the kitchen I saw her coming through the front door with a brown paper bag in her hand. She approached him smiling and they hugged.

Somehow, to this day, it still doesn't make sense to me, but she looked up and noticed me. He never looked my way. Maybe he was pre-occupied with the contents of the paper bag or maybe it was just God's Will. I quietly beckoned for her to come to me and like a robot she walked my way. Luckily, there was a wall blocking our view, the same wall I helped him build.

"Are you busy sweetie, can you talk for a minute" I asked. "Sure" she fearfully mumbled. "Help me climb over this counter please," I asked and she did. I had an urgent sense to get her out of there because I felt he was coming to see where she went. I struggled to get my pregnant belly over the counter before he stopped us from having the conversation that would change the course of my future.

We hurriedly went across the street into McDonald's and the minute I sat down, she spilled the beans. All of them, I didn't have to ask one question. She told me what they did when I was out of town; how he told her he was going to break up with me so they could be together. He told her I was crazy, but she said she didn't believe that because I was so nice to her and she never saw me act crazy.

I looked at her after the final confession and I said, "You do realize I am not only carrying his child, but that he recently asked me to marry him and you are just as guilty as he is." She nodded. I said, "Okay, you are coming back to the club with me and you will be present while I tell him everything you just told me because I don't have time for any 'He said, She said' mess, understood?" She complied.

As we walked back into the club together, the look on his face at the sight of both of us had to be the most priceless thing I had ever seen. To this day I wish I had an I-phone back then to capture that moment. I calmly repeated everything I knew and after each statement I would look at her and say, "Is that correct?"

"Yes" would be her response each time.

My final statement was, "Since this is how things are going to be, I will stay here for a month and work only as a Bartender so I can make enough money to go back to Chicago and have enough time to find my own place in time to have this baby. We are officially done."

I turned to her and said, "You need a ride home?" Even though I declared our break up, I still didn't want to leave those two alone and he didn't want me alone with her any longer so

we took her home. I went back to our place, found a wall to slide down and I had a good, hard cry. I had a cry almost as intense as when my grandmother passed. The pain of betrayal runs deep.

A month later, my friend Trinity came with a guy my mom hired who had a truck, helped me pack my things and take me to my new place where my friend Dock's Mom helped me get in. Within a week, I got a call from Ebony and Jet Magazine's print department asking my availability for a photo shoot. I told them I was eight month's pregnant and they said, "We don't care girl, we only need your face from the chest up, we can crop the rest of the picture.

A month later, I gave birth to a beautiful baby boy who as he got older, I encouraged to have a relationship with his dad. His dad and I co-parented peacefully and throughout the years I did my best to encourage him to have a relationship with his son. That never really happened the way I desired, but I never stood in the way of it. I forgave him for everything to his face and I let go of the past. I can't lie and say that emotional wounds heal as quickly as physical ones because writing this at this moment still stirs up a tad bit of pain and reality of regrets.

I would never regret having my son because he was definitely a blessing. I do regret allowing myself to be in a position where I let someone make me forget who I was and how to love myself more. I thank God I found the "Me" I used to be and I thank Him for saving me from a lifetime of pain.

I've been a victim of bullying, molestation, verbal and physical abuse, betrayal, lies and rumors from all sorts of situations throughout my life, and a victim of my own lack of self-love at one point, but I am no longer the V-word (Victim). Well, at least not that V-word, I am now a Victor and because I am more than a Conqueror, I will always be one. I am now happily married, with two amazing children and I know my self-worth. Sometimes a little prayer goes a long way, just be prepared to hear God's voice when He comes to your rescue.

AMAZING TESTIMONY
by:
FELLA SOUL
Recording Artist and Street Minister
Fellasoul.com

SEEK AND YE SHALL BE FOUND

It started out with me living in Robert Taylors in Chicago, Illinois and watching my mother get abused by my father. She got her skull fractured and her ribs broken. He used to beat on her daily or every other day to the point I can remember her shushing us not to get loud so we could get on the ambulance truck to get away from Robert Taylor's to get away from him. We snuck away and we finally got out of his grasp and then my moms was taking care of us the best way she could, but every time she saw me she saw my father.

I was my father's namesake, the only son with two older sisters. I was the youngest. You would think that I would be spoiled, but it was just the opposite. Anything go wrong in the house, I did it. No matter if I was innocent or not. Whatever I did in school, if I did anything in a show, no one attended, just no type of love. Graduating with good grades, I got no props or respect for it. It drove me to trying to find respect in the streets, I met up with a group of people who always had my back...well, I thought they did. I was smoking weed with them and they just so happened to be the gang, the Vice-Lords. So at the age of eleven, I got a tattoo of the Vice Lords on my arm. I was in the Gardens, the Wild 100's.

I started gangbanging and I bust my first pistol at someone when I was eleven. At the age of twelve I was minister of literature over Vice Lords. No matter what the age group was, I just knew all my literature. I was down, or at least I thought I was down for something, but it was a lost cause. Then, it got worse as time went on. I began doing more and more gangbangin', more and more tattoos, more and more shootins', which led to me being locked up more. I got shot up, stabbed,

and was in and out of prison. I never really made much money. I sold dope, but I always got caught selling. Whatever I did, I got caught. I wasn't like the others so I never really could make much. Bonds were being set higher and higher the more I got locked up. The higher the bond, the more reason I couldn't pay for them, the more I got locked up—even if I didn't get caught for an actual crime.

I found myself going in and out of different religions trying to find God because I found out later that these Vice Lord's that I was so called ruling over, tried to kill me off for a position. Meaning, if they take me out then they take my position, so I found out that there was really no love in the family of some gangs. So, while I'm out on the streets, I just started trying to find God. I searched to find Him through Islam, through Cults and I in all of this wasn't making any money, I mean nothin'. I was just struggling, trying to find God. I finally told God, "Look, since it seems like I ain't gettin' nowhere with you, I'm going to honor the devil and I'm gonna' walk with him."

So, I started poppin' pills, known today as Molly. I was taking all kinds of pills like that, really getting crazy, and eventually going back into the gang banging. I was at a stage in my life where I wasn't caring about anything. Then suddenly, God got me. I got locked up again. God shut me down, but I didn't talk to Him because I didn't want to feel like a hypocrite while I was in jail and letting this be the only reason to start talking to Him. I thought by doing so I would've been more like a hypocrite. Before being released from jail the court officials told me, "You have to pay this fine and if you don't pay this you'll get locked back up."

After being released, I went for what I knew when I was selling crack. As I was walking down the street, in the hood, looking for someone to push the drugs off to, I just threw the dope. I got tired of everything and I said, "God, if I go to jail, then I'm just going to give You glory inside of jail. I'm gonna say if this is where you want me to be then I'm gonna be happy in there, I'm not gonna walk away; I'm gonna be happy." I walked down the street of my block and saw this dude named Eric. He was laying brick and I walked up to him and said, "Do they have anything as far as work, any open jobs?" He said, "It's funny you should ask, I fired seven people yesterday."

He told me to come back tomorrow. Wow, this opportunity was opening up and it was on my block, in my hood and I just felt the presence of the Lord. The next morning about 7 a.m., I sat in his car and he explained to me how the money situation would pay and how he was a pastor and why the blessings were. He started speaking scriptures out of his mouth, but it's not like he was trying to teach me, but it was like, God was teaching me personally. I heard His voice and felt His presence. At the time, I was still part of an occult and had studied everything—Islam, Science, Christianity—so listening to him didn't make me feel like a hypocrite because I felt I had learned everything anyway. He invited me to his church one day and I accepted. He started speaking and God started speaking through him more.

I heard scripture, I heard God's Word, I heard His voice and God told me to memorize the scriptures. I started learning them and God started to pour scriptures into my brain out of the Bible, He started pouring it in my heart and writing it across my heart until I knew over 198 scriptures by memory. I didn't know what these scriptures were when they first got into my body, but when I walked the streets, God spoke to people through me and taught me through me with everything that He placed in my heart. I started going to the brother Eric's church, but I started opening the Bible myself and started letting it pour in me.

I started being more of a hearer and I also became a doer. I started speaking the things He said and walking in what He said walk in. I can remember getting my first car and getting on my knees and saying, "In Jesus Name, I decree I have a car." I would ask Jesus for the car and then believe I had it. I remember walking in my house and telling my family what I had, all the blessings that I had, all my inheritance of Abraham and my gift making room for me and bringing me before great men. I told them how God's word was flowing over me so I could reach millions and allow God to save many through me, as well as God owning cities through me, and everything He told me to decree.

I remember when I told my mom about my first blessing, my car. She started laughing like, "Whatever boy!" "I ain't telling you what I'm going to do, I'm telling what God already did, and I'm standing on it." I had nobody to believe in me. I had no father; nobody taught me how to be a man. No one. God taught me how to be a man. So I stood on it right in her face and told her, "I got it, you don't see it? I'm driving it."

I kept my tongue lined up with what He said I would have and the next month I had a car and my family was like,

"Whoa." I kept speaking, preaching, and decreeing. The music I was writing was secular music and it started changing. It was Hip Hop and R&B still, but with a little Gospel twist because I couldn't stop talking about God, because He was blessing me and I felt His presence.

Time went on and blessings kept continuing to pour in while I was working. I was able to walk away from the construction job and do my gift full time. Then I start touring in a movie with Katt Williams. I was featured on soundtracks, touring for three months, which covered thirty-six states. I remember there were times I had to ask someone for a dollar for cheeseburgers because I didn't have any money, but now, I can buy cheeseburgers for everybody.

God is constantly teaching me that it's not over. I'm not religious; I'm in a relationship, because I fall daily. I fall short and I repent. If you align your tongue up and you believe what God says, He will change you from the inside out. It starts with your tongue. *"Faith cometh by hearing and hearing by the Word of God."* Once you hear it and you start speaking it, 'God-Power' will take over. Don't worry about the fact that you keep falling, cause it ain't gonna matter. All that matters is that you keep this personal relationship and he will continue to change you if you keep repentance in your heart and in your mouth and truly love Him.

Glory Be to God! I'm still walking and I'm still learning and He's still filling me with His Word. I'm still growing and learning how to be a man for Him through the people He places in my life and I will die for my Lord. I ain't gotta fear that because *NO weapon formed against me shall prosper*. Glory Be to God in the Name of Jesus!

AMAZING TESTIMONY
by:
GHERI LEGREE
Fashion Designer/Actress/Singer
JonGheri Couturier
Twitter: @JonGheri

GETTING MY LIFE BACK

I was anxious to get married and my biological clock was ticking. When you're anxious you don't wait for the right one, but you settle for the one you think is the right one. I fell for someone who I thought wanted what I wanted. He was impressed with me being a model, actress, and singer.

Once I got in the marriage, everything changed. What he once thought was impressive soon became a problem and jealousy of my accomplishments set in. The man I met was a facade and nothing like I thought he would be. He was a charming military officer/Baptist preacher that treated me like gold when we dated. He was there financially and emotionally and did whatever it took to get me.

A few months after I married him, I started catching him in lies. I was unaware that he had another relationship right before me and I would soon find out that during our marriage he had several relationships. He would take trips with other women even during my pregnancy with our daughter. The neglect I experienced during my pregnancy was unbelievable.

One morning, while in the hospital, I called to tell him I was hungry and hadn't eaten breakfast and he said he would bring me some food. I did not see him until nine hours later around 6p.m. When he came to the hospital, he sat down and looked at me and said, "I'm too old for this s—t."

I was raised in a Christian home and was taught strong values and morals, especially when it came to marriage. I observed the way my father treated my mother with love, respect, and loyalty so that is the behavior I exhibited as a wife.

I went into my marriage thinking divorce was never an option because I wanted to respect the vows.

From 1992 to 1998 I stayed with a man who cheated and lied because I was too embarrassed of what people might think. I believe I was more in love with the idea of being married than the man I actually married. I began to ask myself was something wrong with me and was I pretty enough? My self-esteem was dying.

Prior to the marriage, I viewed myself as this strong rock with confidence, strength and high self-esteem, but after years of being cheated on, lied to, talked down to, cursed at, dealing with controlling behavior, and female problems due to his extra-marital affairs, I had finally had enough.

My advice to any woman or man would be, don't ever get so caught up in a person that you forget and lose who you are. Never give someone that much power over you because that's not love.

My breaking point was when I found out he was spending money lavishly on other women and taking finances from our household.

The military had honorably discharged him because of an investigation he was under for sexual harassment of twenty-nine women. His behavior had become so erratic I thought he was on drugs, but his addiction was women.

One New Year's Day toward the end of our marriage, my husband posed a question. "Why won't you let me just do what I want to do as long as I come home? My other friend's wives let them do whatever they want as long as they come home."

December of 1997, he and I got into a physical fight while we were driving down the street on the way to the bus station to send me off on tour. I had experienced being cursed at and verbally abused so long that this day was my breaking point. This was the straw that broke the camel's back. Just like Tina and Ike in the movie, *What's Love Got to Do With It?* I lost it and I fought my husband.

After it was over and we said our solemn goodbyes at the bus station all I could think is, no one should ever get you that angry.

While on a national stage-play tour, I became numb from the memory of the years of disrespect and abuse and I realized that divorce was now my option. Today, I thank God that I have rediscovered who I am, who God has designed me to be and now I am a confident, successful and Godly woman. I will never allow anyone to come into my life and disrupt who I am ever again.

Sometimes it takes us going through a situation where someone tells us who we are not, that we finally come out of it knowing who we are. The best thing that came out of me going through all of that hell, was that God still sent me something from Heaven, which is my beautiful, purpose-filled daughter.

There is no greater agony than bearing an untold story inside you.

-Maya Angelou

AMAZING TESTIMONY
by:
MICHELLE ELIZABETH WILLIAMS
Atlanta Georgia
Author of: NOBODY EVER TOLD ME
on Amazon.com and Barnes and Noble
Instagram: @michelleewilliams98

SLEEPING WITH THE ENEMY

My life started out with me being sexually abused by different men and boys. Later, my kid's father who was on crack cocaine really bad would rape me. I started out trying to find love, but it wasn't good. I was with this guy, trying to find a place for me to fit in. My parents were married, but had many adulterous relationships going on.

My father was an alcoholic who beat both me and my mother. My mother was an enabler and she also abused me by shaving my head bald at nine years old for no reason at all. "Your scalp is dead," she said and then shaved my head. It made me think I wasn't pretty enough or I wasn't good enough. When you believe a lie, you cover a lie.

Other kids teased me for years calling me, "The bald headed cook," because my last name was Cook. My father was Indian and black and his mother never liked me or my siblings because we weren't light skinned and didn't have pretty hair. When we would go to her door, she yelled to my father, "Raymond, your Bastard children are here!" My grandmother treated the kids in the neighborhood like they were her own and they referred to her as "Grandmother".

She did love my brother who was her first-born grandchild, but unfortunately he died of Leukemia at the age of seven. It seemed like I was skipped over. She wasn't a grandmother to me or to the rest of my siblings because we weren't light skinned so I didn't know what real love was. She wanted my father to be with a light woman and would say things like, "Go home to your Black B!" She was referring to my mother. My

111

father and his mom didn't get along because she pretended to be his sister for years before he found out the truth. She was a very angry woman.

When I connected with my children's father at eighteen, he was twenty-two and I was trying to be this perfect wife like the *Leave it to Beaver-type*. I started wearing wigs and weaves for years and was afraid to show my husband my real hair because I didn't want him not to love me. I did everything I could to make him love me, all the way down to ironing his socks, cleaned and cooked. I tried to impress upon him that I loved him because I didn't get that as a child, I thought he would love me back and truly fall in love with me.

Instead, he cheated, did crack and cocaine and then one day, I found a letter that exposed he was secretly gay.

I kept it in the back of my mind and didn't tell him because I wanted to keep him. The letter said at the end, "I guess Michelle won," I thought that meant I was a winner and I didn't want to let go because in my mind he chose me over this relationship and that made me love him more because for the first time, someone put me first.

However, his drug and cheating habits, which were growing increasingly worse, caused many arguments and dissention.

Sometimes he would come home so high, I had to drag him up the stairs because he couldn't walk. One night I was only able to pull him into the kitchen and all I could do is wipe his head and pray for him. Many nights he wouldn't even come home. His habit eventually pushed him to sell everything out of our house even down to the food in the freezer.

At the age of twenty, I had a nervous breakdown from all the stress of starving, no food, no money, and the disrespect. My mind left and I snapped for three days. On the first day, I was sitting in school and had been shaking really bad. My hands, and insides were shaking uncontrollably and I was harboring a lot of pain within that filled me up. One particular day, a girl named Christine started crying about some things she was going through and I started crying with her, but didn't know why I was crying. The tears would not stop. Earlier that morning I had plotted and planned to drive my car, with myself and my children, into a tree because I figured that would be the quickest way to kill us. I didn't want to leave my children here with a crack-head or with my parents who had abused me. I felt like I was their only protector. I said, God please don't let me lose my mind and then my mind stopped in a square for 3 days.

I ended up pregnant again with my third child and when I was five months pregnant, he needed drug money and slammed me up against a wall because I would not give him my money. He forcefully took the money and went to get high. I went into pre-mature labor and started dilating as a result of his attack.

The doctors managed to stabilize me and I called my mom because that was the only place I could go. Finally, I left him and moved in with my mom. At the time she was a lover of money, so he called my mother and said he would pay her to rent the room across the hall from the children and me. My mother, knowing we were separated and he was doing drugs agreed to let him come live with us.

After having our third child, he didn't do anything for our newborn even though he was working. He was still spending his money on drugs. I stayed in my room with my children most of the time and stayed away from my husband as much as I could. I was concerned that my mother would hurt my children the way she did me when I was a child. Three months later, I left my mother's home and moved into my own apartment four or five miles away. By this time I had been separated from him for eight months.

Five months after moving into my new place, I was on my couch one night, sleeping and usually slept really good. I woke up at 1:00 a.m. and turned my head to my kids' room and saw a shadow. I called my kids father and he didn't answer. I ran down the stairs and there were hard footsteps behind me and I didn't know who it was, but I ran straight to my sisters apartment downstairs and jumped up on her king size bed.

I saw my ex-husband and ran around in a circle trying to get away from him. My sister was naked so she was struggling to keep the cover on her as we both ran around her room. I ran back into the hallway, something inside me said vomit. I began to heave like I was going to throw up; I started spitting on the floor. "Are you alright, Missy are you alright?" He said. He walked me back up the stairs acting concerned and I didn't realize he had a knife and I was at knifepoint until he made me lie down in the middle of the floor and then he raped me.

"Do you love me?" He had the nerve to ask. I shook my head yes, he said, "No you don't because it don't feel the same. I was going to slit your throat while you were sleep, but I don't do those things anymore." After it was over, I laid there in shock until the next morning. I tried to figure out how he got in so I went on a search of the house checking all the windows and doors and something said, look up. When I did, I saw the attic.

I went up there and found bowls and spoons and books with my kids blankets. He had been secretly living in my attic for two months. For years I lived in fear and to this day I keep my bathroom door closed. He would hang a noose in my closet like he was going to hang himself. He would stalk me at school, standing outside the window. One day, he pushed me and I knocked him so hard in his head a knot rose up. I thought to myself, It's either him or me. So I tore his butt up.

I called the police, but nothing was ever done and they allowed him to get away with everything no matter how many times, he always walked away or was released in one or two hours. I started dating a guy I went to school with and he was very protective of me so he would help run my ex away. Eventually, my ex ended up in jail and thirty years later to this day he is still in and out of jail. He sends hellos through my children from time to time, but I do not respond.

One day in 2004, I got in the shower and denounced every illegal spirit off of me as I washed my body and watched the suds go down the drain. I stepped out of the shower, stepped in front of the mirror, and said, "God, you made Eve for Adam, now please make my husband for me." I reached my hands up to Heaven and I spiritually pulled my future husband down into my loins.

Six months later, Jay Williams walked into my church and he said, "Girl I didn't know you could sing like that, I'll marry you today." The chase was on and even though he lived an hour away, he always found his way to my front door. Eight months later we were engaged and four months after that we were married. It's been the best thirteen years of my life. We never argue.

The first year, however, was very rocky for both of us because we had to learn how to understand each other. We made an agreement and commitment to one another not to hurt one another. He had been cheated on and hurt as well. We had one argument because of miscommunication right before our wedding so we broke up and we got back together. It was a transition because of all I had been through with being abused and cheated on and those things affected us.

We got it together though. We don't argue. We talk about everything. We work together, travel together and he texts me all the time when he leaves to go to work; sweet little texts like,

114

"I miss you already my little sexy." I cry like a baby when he has to spend a day or two away from me because of his work. This is the best love I have ever had and now I know what it truly means to be in love with your best friend. I am definitely VICTORIOUS!

True Love is patient and kind. It is never rude or easily angered

but it always protects, trusts, hopes, perseveres

and it will never fail.

AMAZING TESTIMONY
by:
TONIA TYLER
Motivational Speaker
www.sweetNsocial.com

THE POWER OF FORGIVENESS

I've been married three times and my second marriage is where I had physical abuse. As a woman I thought being married defined success to me, but I didn't realize that success is happiness on the inside and finding your gifts. When we are able to let go of things we've been holding onto; anger, relationship issues, lack of things and frustration, then we're able to find our gifts. I found myself carrying other people's 'bags' that were their responsibility and I had my own 'bags' to deal with.

My second husband and I got married in 2001, separated in 2005 and divorced in 2006. I had been divorced from my first husband several years before I met him. I was tired of being single, we were both in the military, and he was cute so I said, "Hey why not." I recently understood that I was getting married for the wrong reasons. My mom and grandma were married for a long time and I made my decision from the opinion of other people. To travel together we had to be married, but the real reason may not be because we loved each other, but I didn't do what God was giving me in my heart.

I didn't have a relationship with God, I used to think that God was on a cloud floating. I didn't understand why some people got blessed or had the Holy Spirit and others didn't. The first six months, my mother and brother had not known I got married. She was a big influence on me. My son was a year old when we decided to go to the Justice of Peace and for him to be stationed where I had to go, we needed to be married. My mother wasn't crazy about him. They found out after we had some flare-ups and made comments like, "At least you didn't

marry him." Then I said, "Well, neither one of us had a relationship with God," so our experience was just chaotic.

I saw plenty of red flags before we got married, but I did it anyway. My family was more disappointed in the fact that I didn't tell them. We always argued over my son. He threatened to take Kenny and I would get defensive. The first time he hit me, I was holding Kenny and I would say a few things with my sharp tongue and he went for my neck and started to choke me. It was a cycle of every once in a while that we would have these moments. We were both frustrated and there were times he would stomp my head, but we stayed together in spite of it. The full blown out lash was when I swung back with my fist and I knew then we were completely done. Our marriage was over.

My son was four when I found out my ex had another baby that was two years old. He had gotten served with papers and he came home one day and confessed. The mother of the child was in the military as well. I was pissed because my first husband had a child with another woman as well and both of our children were born at the same time. I had told him the worst thing he could do is ever have a child with another woman. Now he had to pay child support and it was very hurtful. He was going to leave the house and I followed him, cussing and going off and he pushed me back then I swung. He choked me and I fell down, he took his shoe and stomped me in my head.

I didn't care because he had already hurt me deeply with this news. I was not completely healed from the pain of my first marriage, in addition, I was dealing with the loss of my mother, and I was overwhelmed. After, we went to a counselor, which we were ordered to do by the military and we told the counselor only about the infidelity, but she knew there was more to the story. The military does not play with domestic violence abuse. They do a full investigation and go into your home and interview your children.

This year is the first time we had a real conversation and he apologized. I knew that I was part of it. The Power of Forgiveness is a blog I wrote. I had to come to a realization that it took two. At that time I didn't know my worth. I know he didn't understand who he was either. It took us ten years to move past it. My son, the youngest child is from my second marriage. In my spirit I felt that his father needed to be more in his life. He started reaching out to me and we were being more civil. One day in the park, I broke down and told him,

"Something inside of me is telling me that you need to be a part of his life. If he wants to live with you I'm okay with that."

He assured me that he wasn't trying to take my son, but he did want to be in his life more. The last drag out fight we had, I said, "It doesn't matter what you do to me physically, you've already killed my spirit." There was nothing else he could do to me. I was done. I was hurt. We were in the military and they said there's no such thing called self-defense. He had a baby with someone-else while we were married. I lashed out at him because of that and he began to hit me. When I swung back at him I knew I was wrong. We went to counseling. He finally admitted that he caused seventy percent of the problem. That's how the door opened for us to make peace.

Now he spends a lot of time with his son. I feel peace and a closure. For a while I didn't want to share this story because I had rank and I didn't want my soldiers to see me as weak. I was embarrassed going through it and I had to put on a strong face because I was in charge of people. Once I came out of it and other women came forward in their abusive relationships, I was able to see things differently. I'm not ashamed of this experience because if it will help someone and they can know that they are not alone then that's why I share. The two of us have forgiven each other and we both individually gained a relationship with God and now we're really good and we co-parent peacefully. We both got the victory.

The battle is not yours, it's the Lord's.

SCRIPTURES ON VICTORY

4 For the Lord your God is the one who goes with you to fight for you against your enemies to give you victory.
Deuteronomy 20:4

13 Therefore put on the full armor of God, so that when the day of evil comes, you may be able to stand your ground, and after you have done everything, to stand.
Ephesians 6:13

57 But thanks be to God! He gives us the victory through our Lord Jesus Christ.
Corinthians 15:57

15 He said: "Listen, King Jehoshaphat and all who live in Judah and Jerusalem! This is what the Lord says to you: 'Do not be afraid or discouraged because of this vast army.
For the battle is not yours, but God's.' "
Chronicles 20:15

19 At the first light of dawn, the king got up and hurried to the lions' den. 20 When he came near the den, he called to Daniel in an anguished voice, "Daniel, servant of the living God, has your God, whom you serve continually, been able to rescue you from the lions?" 21 Daniel answered, "May the king live forever! 22 My God sent his angel, and he shut the mouths of the lions. They have not hurt me, because I was found innocent in his sight. Nor have I ever done any wrong before you, Your Majesty."
Daniel 6:19-22

48 As the Philistine moved closer to attack him, David ran quickly toward the battle line to meet him. 49 Reaching into his bag and taking out a stone, he slung it and struck the Philistine on the forehead. The stone sank into his forehead, and he fell facedown on the ground.
1 Samuel 17:48-49

I fear no evil for He is with me.

CHAPTER 6

DANGERS SEEN AND UNSEEN

I had just gotten off work at a popular pizza parlor in downtown Chicago. It was a late night. I was nineteen years old. My mother was expecting me to go straight home, but I had other plans. I wanted to go see Danny.

I pulled into his neighborhood, but because it was dark, I could not see the addresses. I saw a guy walking down the street. I assumed he was one of Danny's neighbors. Very gullibly, I rolled the window down and asked, "Excuse me, do you know what that address is?" pointing to the curb.

He stopped and asked, "Who you looking for, baby?"
"Danny."

"Yeah, yeah, yeah, that's my boy, he lives right over there." He pointed across the street.

"Thank you."

I parked near where he was pointing. As I pulled in, I noticed he was walking toward my car. Even though I was rolling up the windows on my old school, two-door Lincoln, that my grandmother just bought me, I didn't lock the doors. He came up to the passenger side. Naïvely I thought, *He must need a ride.*

He opened the door and quickly got inside. He looked at me and said, "Drive." His eyes were really glassy, like he was in some trance state. He looked a little on the crazy side or either very high on drugs.

Thinking quickly, I told him, "Danny owes me some money. I'm just going to go get that money and I'll be right back."

I put my hand on the door to open it and he said, "Drive, b**ch, or I'll kill you." He reached into his pocket as if he were pulling out a knife or something. I was too afraid to see it, so I looked away and drove off.

The minute I drove off, I heard a voice, which I believe was either the Holy Spirit or an Angel, say to me calmly, "You have to let someone know what is going on. Make a scene."

As I drove away, he touched me. He put his hand down my shirt and fondled my breasts. I was wearing a short skirt and he put his hand under my skirt and touched my panties. He started noticing my jewelry and began removing each piece. It all happened so fast. It was just a block away from where it all started.

I looked down the street for another car or anything to come. On my left there was a row of houses, but there wasn't anyone around. It was like I was in a deserted area. Then all of a sudden, a pair of headlights came toward me. I had this sense of urgency to let that particular person know that I needed help. Instantly, I braced myself and drove in front of their car. The other driver crashed into me with a look of shock on his face. The guy in the car with me was livid, cussing at me and calling me names. I didn't care. My focus was to get the attention of the driver in the other car. He hit the passenger side of my car where this crazy man was sitting. The driver of the other car was stunned. Unfortunately, I would find out later that he was driving a new car that he had just bought.

I started to physically fight with the crazy guy that was in the car with me. He was mad at me for causing an accident. I jumped up onto the door from inside the car and sat on the window. My arms were flailing outside the car and I was screaming to the top of my lungs, "Help me, help me, oh my God, he's trying to kill me." I was trying to get the driver of the other car to get out of his car and help me.

The crazy guy tried to push me out of the window. I got angry and I punched him in his head! We started tussling with each other as he jumped in my seat and proceeded to try and drive off with me sitting in the window because he couldn't push me out. He tried desperately to drive off, but the car would not move. I was screaming. He was screaming. I felt like I was in a movie scene.

The driver of the other car jumped out, pulled out a gun, pointed it at the crazy guy, and yelled, "Freeze, police!" He was a Cook County Sheriff who had just gotten off duty.

The crazy guy couldn't get out on my side because I was still sitting in the window. He went back to the passenger side, jumped out of the window, climbed over the hood of the Sheriff's car, and dropped all my jewelry on the ground.

I yelled to the Sherriff, "Shoot him! Shoot him!" He responded, "I can't!"

I remember thinking, *Why not?* I knew why. I knew better. My mother was a police officer and protocol was you couldn't shoot someone in the back. Well, that was the rule back in the day. It's hard to tell what the rules are now. However, at that moment, I wanted him to shoot this man in the leg or something to stop him so he wouldn't do the same thing or something worse to someone else.

The crazy guy got away. He wasn't even running. He was jogging across the street. I watched him disappear in the darkness and get away.

The driver of the other car confessed that he thought it was a staged hijacking, which is why he delayed in helping me. He apologized and said, "I thought you guys were trying to scam me. I thought you were trying to carjack me."

People started coming out of their homes. A lady asked, "Baby, you okay? I heard you screaming all the way down the street. I live two blocks away and I heard you screaming."

I thought to myself, You heard me and you are just now coming out?! Thank you.

Someone else said, "I wasn't coming out there with that crazy man."

I had this conversation over and over with different people. The block was now filled with people. Some of them confessed that they were in their windows watching. Not one person called the police.

We called or had someone to call the police.

Finally, Danny came out. He heard me, too. He said he didn't know it was me.

I said, "You knew I was coming to visit. You should've been looking out for me."

I called my mother and told her what happened. She said, "Sure, Trisha, sure. You're coming home this late because you've been out doing something."

"No, really, Mom."

She did not believe me until I made it home with the police report. When I walked through the door and handed it to her she broke down in tears of relief. She knew what had been happening to a lot of young ladies at that time and realized it could have happened to me. Dan Ryan Woods was a place where women's dead bodies were being found weekly. Many of them had been raped. I was near that area.

I knew in my spirit that drugged up or crazy man was going to rape me and possibly kill me. I knew he had evil intentions the minute I looked into his eyes.

The next day, because my car was still there, my mother drove me out that way to see the car and look for the criminal. She wanted to see how much damage had been done to my car and she really wanted to try to find the man that had jumped in my car. I did not think that would happen. I thought, *There is no way in the world we are going to find this guy.*

She saw another fellow officer who I thought was arresting a guy. She knew the officer and I just happen to know the guy I assumed was being arrested. She told the officer what happened the night before. He said he would look around as soon as he was finished.

As we were driving and passing by men, my mother kept asking, "Is that him?"

And I would say, "No, Mom, that's not him."

About a block later, I saw a guy that fit the exact description of the guy from the night before who jumped in my car.

This guy was carrying a small brown paper bag. I remembered at that moment that the crazy man had a small brown bag, too.

So I said, "I think that's him." "Trisha, are you sure?"

"Yes, I think that's him."

In fact, the guy actually looked at us, and he looked nervous. He saw me looking at him. He looked directly into my eyes. He didn't have that same glassy look like the night before though.

My mother made a U-turn in the middle of the street and went back to the on-duty police officer. He followed us back to find this guy. We caught up with him walking. He had made it another block or so. We turned left in front of him, just like most police do when they catch someone they have been looking for. They pinned him in and my mother and the officer jumped out of the car.

The officer pulled his weapon and they were yelling, "Get down!

Get down right now!"

The guy was asking, "What did I do? What'd I do?"

He was shaking and he had his hands up. He got on the ground. He looked up at me and started crying, "Ma'am, please, whatever it was I didn't do it. I have a family. I didn't do it."

The man was crying so hard I started crying, too. Now I was confused. I was unsure.

My mother told me, "You better get it together and get it together fast. This is what they do. They act like they didn't do it and they cry crocodile tears to make you feel sorry for them. Don't you believe that bull crap!"

The next thing I knew, there was a woman walking down the street. She came out of nowhere straight toward me. I think she was holding a *Watch Tower* magazine. I thought that was odd because she was alone. Normally, when you see a Jehovah's Witness they are in pairs or groups. In a very calm voice she said, "Daughter, what's wrong?"

Through my tears I gave her a brief synopsis of what had happened the night before and what was happening right then with this man on the ground. She seemed completely unfazed by the drama unfolding right there in front of us. I just felt like it was okay to talk to her. I was friendly anyway, but it was something about her that made me feel comfortable. I was so young and gullible. I knew my mother was zoned in on catching this guy, so it was nice to have a compassionate ear to hear what I was saying.

My mother and the other officer were taking care of business. They scared me.

I told the lady, "I'm not sure that's the guy that got in my car last night."

The lady said, "Trust me, when the time is right, God will reveal it to you." Then she gave me a sweet smile and walked away.

We went to the police station. I remember the detective telling me that this man had a rap sheet and that he had done some things. "All you have to do is say the word," he said.

I said, "I can't say the word if I'm not one hundred percent sure that this is the man that jumped in my car last night. I don't want to send an innocent man to jail."

The detective said, "Trust us. He's not as innocent as you think. He has done a lot of things."

I could sense that I irritated the detective because it seemed like they just wanted me to say, "He's the one.'" They wanted to book him and put him in jail.

I said, "I have to be sure."

So they said, "Fine. We have some pictures for you to look at." That didn't help.

Then there was a lineup.

They said, "We're going to put him alongside some other guys and we need you to decide if this is the man or not. We really think it's the man."

They took me to the room to view the lineup. Right before I entered the room, the face of the guy from the night before flashed right before my face. Just like the lady told me that when the time was right, God would reveal it to me.

When I looked at the man in the lineup, I realized it was not the right man.

The person in lockup was not the man that had been in my car, but for some reason, I did feel that the wrong guy being arrested was experiencing a divine intervention that was necessary for him. It was as if he had done, or was about to do something he shouldn't have and this experience was going to help him straighten up and fly right.

The whole thing also stopped me from doing something that I shouldn't have been doing in the first place. It interrupted me from being with a guy, possibly getting pregnant, or even catching an STD. Who knows? I was trying to hook up with Danny for the wrong reasons.

Now my car was totaled and I had to pay to repair the officer's car I hit. Well, actually my mother paid and I was grateful. I'm also grateful I am still alive. I'm healed, but there is always some degree of trauma when you experience something like that. For years, I would immediately lock my doors when I got in the car. Honestly, I still do.

These days, I'm more guarded and careful of talking to strangers. My husband laughs at me because I still lock the door if he leaves me in a running car, if only for a minute.

Sometimes when I think back on that day, I recall how the lady that came out of nowhere was so calm and had nothing but words of encouragement for me. I wonder if she was an angel coming to comfort me. I will always remember how her peaceful voice, calm demeanor, and compassion for my well-being really meant a lot. I stopped crying just being able to talk

to her and as we drove down the street to the police station, I searched for her but didn't see her walking anywhere.

I am also very grateful that the man got out of the other car with a gun to help. I'm grateful that he had the courage to do it. He really thought we were trying to hurt him, yet he still responded.

I think about the many women before and after me that have been put in that situation by someone touching them inappropriately or threatening their lives. There have been so many people carjacked, raped and even murdered.

The neighbors who stayed behind their peepholes and watched the incident through their windows, heard me screaming, crying, saw me hanging out of the car, begging the driver of the car I ran in front of for help, and they all waited until the crazy man ran off before they came out or called the police. They watched as if they had a bag of popcorn and they were looking at a movie.

The neighbors could have responded faster, and called for help, or just come out of their homes. I understand they were concerned for their safety, but they could have done something. They could have called one another and decided to open their doors or make some noise to scare him off. There is power in numbers.

I'm so different than that. If I see someone in distress I immediately go into resolution mode. How can I help? What can I do? Who can I call? I'm not going to just stand there watching. They need help. I would have tried to do something. Sometimes we have to take a stand boldly, especially when we know we have the protection of God in our lives. We have to stand up. In spite of that man touching me, and taking my jewelry, I knew I was going to be okay. I just didn't know how it was going to play out. I knew God was with me.

AMAZING TESTIMONY
by:
CHRISTOPHER WILLIAMS
Graphic Designer of
Amazing Testimonies

BLOW OUT

About twenty years ago, I was driving on the highway in a 1979 Capris Classic, blue and rusty, and my wife at the time and three children were in the car. The tire blew out and my car went from facing forward to facing backward in that lane.

I was in front of an eighteen-wheeler truck when it happened. My car did a 360, but at the 180 point I saw the truck driver's shocked expression, we were face to face. He looked as if he didn't know what he was going to do.

I was in the right lane on the expressway and a lane had just begun to merge to the right. My rear right tire blew out, sending the car on that amazing, miraculous 360 spin. At the 180 point of that spin, I was still in my lane, looking directly at the eighteen-wheeler truck driver who was behind me. Miraculously, God's Angel pushed my car out of my lane and also out of the merging lane and my car rested facing forward on the shoulder of the expressway.

After the car rested for ten seconds or so, my wife said, "Whew! I'm sure glad you were driving," but it was really God's Angel's saving us from calamity because I don't recall doing anything skillful driving wise or anything miraculous on my part. My car went all the way to the right facing two lanes, to all the way facing forward. It was definitely God's Angels.

AMAZING TESTIMONY
by:
BOB SUMNER
Partner at Laugh Mob Enterprises
Producer of the critically acclaimed,
HBO's Russell Simmons Def Comedy Jam
Instagram: @Bobsumner24

LEFT FOR DEAD

For me, December 14, 2005 was a day to celebrate. It was a day I was at my Uncle Robert's bar and his brother James was there. We were celebrating the beginning of the holiday season and the three of us were there together, joyous and happy and it was time to start the celebration. My Uncle decided to close his bar, The Omega Lounge, for the night due to the frigid weather. We decided to go to Mike's Tavern, the popular local hangout. It was freezing cold, twelve degrees and windy.

We arrived at Mikes Tavern, went in, took some seats and were about to have a toast. A local guy and friend of the bar from the neighborhood came in looking for a ride to go to Newark, New Jersey, so he asked me if I could give him a ride and I told him if he hung around I would because I knew the area. I noticed he continued to ask other people for a ride, which was fine with me because we weren't going until I got ready.

It was so cold that night and no one was going that way but me. He even asked if I needed gas money and I said, "No, I'm good." We got in the car and were driving on the Garden State Parkway. On the way there, he tried to give me directions that I didn't need and then he started telling me about this girl he was seeing and I was taking him to her. His phone rang and it was her. It was 10:30 at night and the liquor stores were closed. She wanted me to take them to the bootleg spot. I said, "I can drop you off, but I can't wait, we gotta keep it moving." She wanted to go also and I agreed to pick her up, the whole time he was trying to give me directions, but I already knew where we were going because it was near my school that I attended, Seton Hall University. She called again and as I think back to that moment, a red flag should've gone up, but it didn't.

When we turned down Boylan Street, which I knew was a one- way street. I pulled over on the side in my silver Escalade and up to her house. She didn't come to the truck, which I found weird because she had just called and he told her what kind of car we were in. I told him I had to get out and let her know it was us, but at that moment she jumped into the back seat directly behind me. When I spoke to her, she didn't say a word.

I'm sitting there and the guy I was giving a ride to ran and opened up the door to get back into the passenger seat, as he was about to sit down, a guy came behind him and put a .9-millimeter in his back. She still had yet to utter a word. The man with the gun walked my male passenger in front of my truck and they disappeared on the side of a house. In the meantime, I didn't want to pull off because I didn't want to leave him and I wasn't sure what she was up to because she was still behind me. I was willing to deal with whatever was about to go down and face the consequences.

My car door was still open and she was still behind me. It was hot in my car and I didn't have my jacket on because the heat was on, but freezing outside, I had a brand new special edition Jam Master Jay, Phat Pharm cell phone that I was quite proud of in my hand. I looked to the left and four guys, three with ski masks, ran up to my car, and opened the driver's side door. I asked her, "What's going on?" She didn't respond. One of the guys had a sawed off shotgun pointed at my head. He hit me with the butt of the gun and the guy without a mask hit me in my face.

The rest of the guys joined in and started to hit me in my head and face multiple times until I fell out of the car and then they continued to beat and stomp me down. Right before they attacked me, I felt a warm sensation go down my legs and realized at that moment that I had urinated on myself. Thank God though for my athleticism which helped me to use the old 'crabbing' football technique to get away from them and into the middle of the street. I then put my hands up and continued to back up because I knew that South Orange Avenue was a main intersection and I refused to let them shoot me in my back.

I was scared for my life. My eyes and face were swollen and bloody. I was freezing, but blood was gushing profusely from my head. I would later realize that there was a hole the size of a quarter in my head. I needed to tie my head up with my shirt making a decision to either catch pneumonia or bleed to death. I was so scared that they were still coming after me and I got a mile and a half away and saw a guy taking out garbage. I approached him for help. He looked at me like I was a crack head and he knew I was desperate. He went upstairs and got a hoodie for me to put on and a phone for me to use. I was in the midst of calling my friend, Hassan, who worked at the gas station near where I was attacked when a police car rode up to me with my male passenger in the back seat pointing at me saying, "There he is!" When the police saw the terrible condition that I was in, they immediately called an ambulance that took me to University Hospital Trauma Unit.

The trauma unit was terrifying. While there, the homicide division came to get my police report and at the same time I'm giving the report, I was getting staples in my head. I was being patched up while recalling this horrible ordeal. I came to find out that the young lady who got in my car is the one who set me up to be attacked. I would find out that she only knew my male passenger through My Space and she had planned to set up whoever he was getting a ride from.

I honor my Dear Lord and Savior for helping me get out of this ordeal. My truck was found twenty-eight days later from being towed. Weed, liquor, jackets, and women's phone numbers were found in my truck from where the guys had fun joyriding in it. The person that helped me by following through with my case and retrieved my vehicle was a councilman at the time and now he is the mayor of the city of Newark, Ras J. Baraka. Without his and God's help, I was a lost cause.

Retaliation and vengeance were thoughts from the pain these men caused me but God's grace and peace kept me from repaying wrong with wrong. December 14, 2016 will mark eleven years that this has happened to me and I have thought about this incident every single day for the past eleven years. Three years after the incident, I had become so close to God and at some point, I wanted my birthday to be extra special and on that third year, my birthday fell on a Sunday and I got baptized. I am now healed and a better man, life has become simple because I know who my God is.

Today I ask for and receive Your Grace Lord.

AMAZING TESTIMONY
by:
VINCENT C. WALKER *and* MOTHER CARRIE RICHARDS
Singer/Music Producer/Former member of R. Kelly and MGM
Mother of Mountain Moving Faith Church International
Instagram: @gigginvince68

LOST AND FOUND

Carrie:

Vince was two years old at the time and we were living in my Great Uncle's home in West Oakland, California. The lock on the front door was broken and I told my uncle to fix it, but he had not yet fixed it. I know God takes care of us even when we don't have a lock on the door, but I didn't know how to do it myself. I put Vince to bed to take a nap and his one-month old sister was already asleep. Vince decided he wanted to go sightseeing and he got up and just walked out of the house.

I woke up and realized he was gone. I looked all over the house and couldn't find him, I went upstairs looking for him at the neighbors who hadn't seen him either, and then I panicked. The worst thoughts went through my mind. There was a picture in my mind that Vince was walking on the expressway and it terrified me. What could have happened to my two year old? I called the police department and then I called my grandmother who lived in East Oakland and told her what happened. When the police came, they searched the trashcan, the back yard, even went through all the rooms and there was no sign of him.

I was frustrated with them for wasting time looking in small trashcans because Vince was tall and too big to fit in that can. I get irritated when I even talk about it. I felt like it was a racial profiling thing to do. Usually they say you have to wait 24 hours to deem someone missing. I was screaming and hollering so much that they decided to act immediately in helping me find him. They posted his picture at bus stops, taxicab stands and taxi-drivers had them. They even talked about him being missing on the news.

Vince:

Grandma, also known as 'Mama Mae', told me I used to go to church with my great grandmother, also known as 'Mother', every Sunday. She said that my mom would meet her and she would take me to church with her on Sunday. The day I was missing was a Sunday. She thought I was trying to go meet her so I could go to church. I talked to Mama Mae about this a year before she passed. She said, "Great Grandma thought you knew that the time had passed for you to go to church and your mom was taking too long, so you just left the house." I know that's deep, but that's what she said.

Carrie:

You ain't lying, that's a little too deep for me.

Vince:

I've seen the newspaper clippings, that my sister had drawn a mustache on my picture since and I really don't remember any details about the incident, but when I saw the article, I was in third or fourth grade and I asked my mother about the details. She said, "What y'all doing in my pictures?" I think we got in trouble for putting the mustaches on there.

Carrie:

You know you did. My grandmother, also known as 'Mother', came and she was there while the police were there. She was torn apart and I know she was thinking it was foul play on my part, but when I explained it to her, she began to console me. I didn't get any sleep that night and the neighbor watched my baby for me because I was so stressed out. At 8:00 a.m. the next morning, I went outside. I was talking to a policeman who was standing on my right. When I looked down the street to my left, I saw a glimpse of the outfit that Vince had on the day before. It was a one piece short set with no sleeves and the top was white with a blue sailboat on it. The shorts were red.

I recognized the outfit right away. As I was talking to the cop, I said, "I think that's him right there."

"Are you sure?" he said. I said, "Yes!"

Vince was with a man who was an older, tall, black man with gray hair on his face and head. It appeared that the man had stayed up all night.

The policeman said, "Are you sure that's your child?"

I said, "Yes! Look at the picture!" I broke out running straight to my son and Vince ran to me. He was really glad to

see me and I picked him up, kissed him and I cried, thanking God.

The cop said to the man, "What are you doing with this child?" He said, "I found this kid in the park. I saw him walking by himself and I kept him with me all night while I played cards. I saw the kid all on the news and I knew he was missing."

The park was three streets from my house and there was a main street that Vince had to cross to get to it. The man thought it was a ransom for Vince's return and expected some money.

The cop was very upset and said, "You did what?"

He wanted to lock the man up, but I said, "Can you please get my son to a hospital so we can check him out?"

The policeman let the man go and called the ambulance. We had a German Shepard named King who loved Vince and when King realized Vince had returned, he chased the ambulance all the way to the hospital, which wasn't close. When we arrived to the hospital, King was tired from running. I told King he had to sit and wait, because he couldn't come in. I told him to stay and he was obedient because he was sitting right there when we came out. It appeared, thank God, that someone had given him water.

Inside the hospital, they checked Vince for scratches, bruises, cuts, and possible sexual abuse. It was a blessing that he was perfectly fine. When we got ready to leave, we had to catch a cab home and I had to explain to the cab driver what happened with Vince and begged the man to let King ride home with us. He agreed and I gave him some extra money for bringing us all home. People started sending me encouraging letters in the mail telling me they were happy for me that Vince returned and they were blessed by the story they saw on the news and in the papers. That is one moment of my life that I would never want to relive. In spite of it all, God still took care of us and I am so grateful.

SCRIPTURES OF PROTECTION

---

³ *But the Lord is faithful, and he will strengthen you*
and protect you from the evil one.
2 Thessalonians 3:3

¹ *Have mercy on me, my God, have mercy on me, for in you I take*
refuge. I will take refuge in the shadow of your wings
until the disaster has passed.
Psalms 57:1

⁴ *Keep me safe, Lord, from the hands of the wicked; protect me from*
the violent, who devise ways to trip my feet.
Psalms 140:4

¹⁹ *The righteous person may have many troubles, but the Lord delivers*
him from them all.
Psalms 34:19

¹⁷ *The wicked go down to the realm of the dead,*
all the nations that forget God.
Psalms 9:17

¹⁰ *So do not fear, for I am with you; do not be dismayed, for I am your*
God. I will strengthen you and help you; I will uphold
you with my righteous right hand.
Isaiah 41:10

⁴ *Even though I walk through the darkest valley, I will fear no evil, for*
you are with me; your rod and your staff, they comfort me.
Psalms 23:4

⁸ *The Lord will watch over your coming and going*
both now and forevermore.
Psalms 121:8

He's my protector, my provider, and my everything.

CHAPTER 7

EAGER ENTREPRENEURS TO SUCCESSFUL BUSINESS OWNERS

I once had a cleaning business with my friend Janet and we called it Sister to Sister Cleaning. We went through the process of planning it with our notes, ideas, and suggestions and then we got our DBA (Doing Business As) so we could open a bank account in the company's name. It was a very exciting time and then we made the flyers and put our ads in newspapers. At first things seemed really slow, but gradually picked up.

Our customers multiplied and were scattered all over the Los Angeles area. We had even gotten some homes on a regular basis. Finally, we were making money and calling our own shots and then the big contract came with a building of 600 apartments. Every time someone moved out, we had an apartment to prepare for the new tenants. My daughter was a baby at the time and my son was very young. Janet also had a young daughter, so conflicts of trying to pick them up or drop them off or sometimes bring them with us soon arose.

The business was slightly interfering with my ability to do auditions, but we were under contract and had to do what we had to do. Then, we saw roaches coming out of the cabinets in full force at the building we were contracted at. The one thing I hate besides Satan himself, are roaches. These suckers were big too, and the final straw was taking them home in our cars and in our cleaning buckets. I was so busy cleaning other people's homes and offices that I didn't have time to clean my own.

The reality of having our own business was starting to kick in and the mutual decision to dissolve SISTER TO SISTER happened. I knew in my heart that my focus was the entertainment business and my partner and I dreamed of the day we would be able to hire other people to do the work for us, but that would take more money and another phase of paperwork and hard work. It was disappointing and surely we

didn't want to be another statistic that says eight out of ten entrepreneurs don't succeed.

I am honored to present to you testimonies of a few faithful and determined people, who fought through adversity and now are very successful business owners.

---

here are only two ways to live your life. One is as though nothing is a miracle. The other is as though everything is a miracle.

- Albert Einstein

AMAZING TESTIMONY
by:
DEBRA HUBBARD
CEO of Black Don't Crack apparel
www.blackdontcrack.com

BLACK DON'T CRACK

After being married for sixteen years I seemed to have vanished in the midst of being a wife and doing all of my motherly obligations. I dealt with the typical things that most married couples had to cope with in relationships. However, the most unbelievable and tormenting for me was being physically, mentally, and verbally abused. The pain of the destruction of my family haunted me for years. I had grown to be so weary and depressed that my life was spiraling out of control and I felt there was no way out. I found myself at fifty years old dealing with new dynamics that were breaking down my self-esteem and it really started to destroy the strong black woman that I knew myself to be. My struggle of having to reinvent myself wasn't easy. The pressure of trying to keep up the lifestyle to which I was accustomed was an uphill battle. Having to deal with my daughter being in college and having two sons in high school and junior high was a pressure within itself. Not knowing where the money was coming from to up keep my bills and making sure there was food on the table was a challenge. Things I may have taken for granted mattered more than ever. I found myself at a crossroads in my life and I had to make some life-changing decisions to try to reinvent myself. At this point, I was ready to give up or roll over and die.

I recall one day falling to my knees in my bedroom, weeping, begging, and confessing to God that I needed a miracle to make me believe in myself again! I remember my mother always saying that God works in mysterious ways. I recall going out one night and meeting a man who was enamored with my physical beauty for my age. He said, "YOU ARE BLACK DON'T CRACK!" This old adage is associated with looking good for your age. It was at that moment I

realized that God had connected the dots and He gave me my miracle.

Those dark and black moments I experienced in my life were just a brief setback for a setup for success, as my pastor often preached. God revealed to me that I was created to overcome those black and dark moments. This also made me realize that this is not only unique to adulthood, but all ages can experience pain, fear, and uncertainty. For example, I remember being fearful as a child. We moved to a predominately white community when I was six years old. I think about the racism I experienced being so young. We were the first and only black family to attend Our Lady of Grace, a Catholic elementary school in Somerdale, New Jersey. We were also the only black family in our neighborhood. I remember as a child strolling to the store and a car passed by me and threw two cards out the window. I waited for the car to get out of my sight before I ran over to pick up the cards. It read: *You have just been paid a visit by the Ku Klux Klan! Would you like a real visit?* Also, it had a drawing of three hooded figures on the card. I remember running home and telling my mother about the cards. She became extremely alarmed. She questioned me about where I got the cards from and she asked me if I noticed if anyone followed me home. I told her how three white men in a car drove away after they dropped the cards. When she explained the meaning of the message on the card of being a death threat then I became very afraid. She saw that I was terrified and upset and she assured me that God would protect me always. I believed her wholeheartedly and felt comforted by her words.

Reflecting on the trials and tribulations I endured truly birthed my passion and purpose that led me to God's destiny for my life, giving me the vision that I was made to inspire. With my inspirational apparel line, I travel the globe to bring hope to the hopeless by identifying with people experiencing pain similar to mine. I remind them that Black Don't Crack! This is a universal message that transcends all races, colors, and creeds. "Black Don't Crack" is a *Triumphant Movement about Strength and Determination through Adversity*.

The Black Don't Crack brand has been a blessing with giving me many opportunities that still make me shake my head. A brand that didn't start up with a lot of money but plenty of heart. Speaking of heart, Kevin Hart was one of the first celebrities to wear our Black Don't Crack T-shirt on

141

television, debuting on *The Real Husbands of Hollywood*. We are so thankful for the notoriety that we still receive from that product placement on that show. Tri-Destined films has collaborated with best-selling author Carl Weber to showcase his novels, *The Man In 3B, The Preacher's Son,* and *The Choir Director* on the big screen, featuring our T-shirts. We are also proud to mention and thank a host of other celebrities that sport our Inspirational Apparel line: Vanessa Bell Calloway, Christian Keyes, Christopher Spencer, Dorien Wilson, Kathy Sledge, Blair Underwood, Kim Kimble, Natalie Cole, Kel Mitchel, Kim Coles, Vanessa Williams, Bilal, Jussie Smollett, YoYo, Jo Marie Payton, Telma Hopkins, Carla Hall, Tony Grant, Trisha Mann-Grant, and a host of others.

In closing, I encourage you to visit our website (www.blackdontcrack.com) and purchase a Black Don't Crack T- Shirt to support our movement. This makes a great gift for someone that has inspired you or who represents the Black Don't Crack mantra.

There are no secrets to success, it is the result of preparation, hard work and

learning from failure.

-Colin Powell

AMAZING TESTIMONY
by:
HONORABLE TAMMY COLLINS MARKEE RCC
Executive Producer of The Garnett Celebrity Newsletter
Author of Gain from the Pain and The Polish Shaft
Business Manager for Voice America Network; Live the Life,
Live the dream
Ambassador Referral Agent for Kish Magazine.
www.kish-magazine.com

HURRICANE KATRINA AFTERMATH

This is a High-Spirited moment for me to share my testimony because it's my first time.

God had prepared me for the death of my twenty-five-year-old younger sister, Dr. Twanna Collins who had sickle cell anemia. She was hospitalized many times over the years because of the crisis. I would sit in the hospital next to her bedside many times asking, "What can I do to take the pain away?" God said, "Just pray."

Many times she would get better, but the disease was still there. She was born with this sickness and one day after seeing her in and out of the hospital since her birth I just prayed for God's Will to be done. God's Will was to take her to her heavenly home where there was no more sickness.

That was a dark time in my life, losing my sister. I experienced much sadness, emotional stress, and unanswered questions. For someone who had been in my life since childhood, that was quite devastating and the first year I mourned the hardest. She shared so many memories with me and we had an extensive family history.

When death robs you of your loved one, it seems unfair, untimely, and devastating.

One day, I was visiting my sister's gravesite and there was a man there in the same area visiting his grandmother's grave and we struck up a conversation. He was really burdened and I was still grieving, but it was in my spirit to pray for this man.

143

After I prayed for him and left that cemetery, the dead weight of me mourning my sister, fell off of me at that moment and I left it there.

That's why I tell people, I have risen from the ashes. I had been struggling with my ministry, I had gone into a shell and wasn't talking to people like I used to until I met this man. God wanted me to press through that and realize that her body is gone, but her spirit lives on and I would see her again. With me being obedient and praying for that man, the graveyard clothes fell off of me and were buried there.

I had to learn that longsuffering has the noble ability to outlive any anguish that we may suffer and I knew that through it all God was a very present help in the time of trouble. It was an element in redefining my faith and I learned how to be totally fixated on God. I was experiencing so much pain and debilitating hurt and I felt like I was in a cage of oppression.

Then an ironic twist in my life came. Hurricane Katrina hit the city of New Orleans. I was born and raised there so I had quite a few family members there as well; it would be five days after the hurricane hit that I would see or speak to them. That catastrophic event during the stormy time in my life, God had prepared me for all of the seasons of loss that I went through.

I am a Hurricane Katrina survivor and I can relate to other survivors. I know about the sense of survivorship. When it hit, I was still in the city. Two elderly people, a couple that had been married for over fifty years needed my assistance, so I stayed behind. I saw the homelessness, the hunger, debris, devastation and the looting in different stores—stealing shoes, clothes and food.

Some people that were actually healthy now have mental issues. I talked to someone who never had a series of depression and was clinically labeled bi-polar after Hurricane Katrina. We were considered like a third world country because we already had a homeless problem before the catastrophe. The city will never be the same even though it has been many years. I wound up in a homeless shelter with the elderly couple, Mr. and Mrs. Boothe.

A woman opened her home up to us. To have a stranger open and trust you in their home was wonderful. I lost everything and I had to pray and do a lot of fasting. I saw looting and caskets floating down the street. It was so much devastation it almost looked like the world was coming to an

end. I was trying to have a peace of mind with all the chaos surrounding me.

Even through trying to build that bridge of love through helping the couple and praying with others, I learned how to build a bridge of love with those I encountered through life. It is for our fellow man to build that bridge and it was for me to answer the call of doing that beyond all of the rumble happening in the city. To not allow the circumstances to disorient me, and not to allow the enemy's plan to circumvent the work that God planned in my life.

My love for God was to be used as a catalyst because I saw the great lost and I needed to help others overcome their fears and phobia's. I encouraged them to hold on and people at the point of death, I prayed for. There was one older lady in her early eighties who was handicapped and she got real sick and had a problem with breathing. She didn't have her medication and I assured her to hold on because help was on the way. She was very weak and could barely glance at me, but she said, "Thank you baby, I appreciate that and I trust God."

One young lady in her twenties was frantic and said she was having a panic attack. She said she had to get out of there because it was too much. I calmed her down and told her, "God is going to get us out of here." I made her take deep breaths and she told me she would be okay. I will never know how or if they survived because eventually I was evacuated on the bus and left the city. It was a sense of relief that I was able to get the elderly people out of there, but I felt some emotional stress because we had to leave others behind. As I rode off, I couldn't believe what I was seeing. I looked back and thought, *I can't believe this*. This is just not real. A lot of people in New Orleans never left the city. They were stuck. No car, credit cards, nothing. My family came into my thoughts because I knew they were worried about me because I was in the heart of New Orleans. No one had phone service, but after a few days we realized the power of text messages. I was on the bus thinking, *What next? Where do I go from here?*

Once the rescuers came, they told us they were taking us to Baton Rouge, Louisiana. I wasn't crazy about Baton Rouge, but I had no choice in the matter. I was just grateful that the elderly couple that had been with me made it out okay and I was thanking God for my life. I was in Baton Rouge for about a month. I stayed in a shelter for one day and then citizens of

Baton Rouge and other nearby areas, started taking all the displaced people into their homes.

I ended up staying at a woman's home, Mrs. Bennie Harry; she was a Christian. Her son was a Pastor and she lived in Zachary, Louisiana. She was very kind-hearted. Her house was clean, she prepared meals for us, and she let me drive her car. Mrs. Harry was a widow and one of the sweetest women I have ever met. One day, Mrs. Harry said, "Come see this bad car accident on TV!" I looked at the television and said, "Wow that's a bad accident." Seconds later, I noticed that it was my first cousin, Harry Collins Jr. and he was one of the cleanup crew for the Hurricane and now he was killed from a blowout on the freeway.

The elderly couple stayed in the home as well. They were in their eighties. I stayed there for one month before I was able to get back to New Orleans and check my own home. When I returned, everything had molded. I lost everything. What really hurt more than losing the material things was losing my precious momentums. I wanted to salvage all of my heirlooms and memories, but I couldn't. My house was damaged beyond control with eight feet of water.

Thank God for FEMA who came and did the repairs to my home. It took about six months to get my house back in shape and the city was basically deserted.

During the restoration period, I moved to North Carolina and had my own place there for a year. At the time I had a business and with that revenue and FEMA's help I maintained living in North Carolina. I decided to move to Houston because I wanted to start somewhere new with better opportunities at the time. I checked back in with my elderly friends and they were doing well. I made sure they were also able to get back to New Orleans and settled in their home.

After moving to Texas, I was able to connect with new people and I met Mr. Leonard Chaikind, an institutional investor who I mentor and my life started looking up. I also met people in the business and entertainment arena. I was asked to participate in various projects dealing with film projects, real estate, and civil rights movements. I was ordained as an Evangelist in 2006 after the Hurricane after having my license for eighteen years prior to that.

In Texas, I started a deliverance ministry for people dealing with depression, mental illness, oppression, and physical illnesses as well. God gave me a gift for healing. Years ago, I

was at a church and a man was praying, he fell out and wasn't breathing. Everyone was upset because they were close to him. My co-worker tried to stop me from praying for him. She said, "No don't go, don't go, you're going to disturb the order of the church."

At the time, it was a traditional Baptist church in Lockport, Louisiana that didn't believe in the laying on of hands nor did they approve of speaking in tongues. The Gifts of the Spirit was not accepted, but I said, "I have to go." I walked up to the altar in front of everybody and I said, "Church we have to pray. Stretch your hands forward and pray." I then laid my hands on his chest and the paramedics came in at that time and said, "He's not breathing." I reached back to the man and prayed over him again and said, "In the Name of Jesus," before I could continue the prayer, the man immediately started breathing again. The paramedics looked in awe, but the pastor and the church were more amazed. The pastor looked at me and said, "I have to get my church more into The Gifts."

He began teachings on The Gifts of the Holy Spirit after that experience. I realized that even though I've had reoccurring hurt patterns through my life, God has given me resilience to break through those walls with tenacity. I also realize that Hope begets Hope and all of my experiences have helped and influenced my ministry, my business, and my personal life. I had been praying for so long, but I found out that God answers when He wants to answer. I felt like deliverance ministry was so difficult, but God works behind the scenes.

One day, he sent a man of God that said, "You have to launch out into the deep." I needed a bigger platform. The late, Denise Matthews A.K.A. 'Vanity' was on Dr. Yomi Barnett's radio show and I did a tribute to her life on the air, which opened up the opportunity for me to give her an inspirational message. Soon I would have that opportunity with others like Bunny DeBarge and Jeff Clanagan with Code Black Films. Through the show and magazine platforms, I was able to get the word out. Media has such an influence over the hearts and minds of people so I was excited when Dr. Kishma George presented Kish Magazine to me and I would be able to interview people from all walks of life.

We have to learn how to successfully transfer ourselves from the cage of oppression and through that we can help ourselves by starting the gain from the pain.

SCRIPTURES ON SUCCESS

---

¹³ *I can do all things through Christ who strengthens me.*
Philippians 4:13

⁴ *Take delight in the Lord,*
and he will give you the desires of your heart.
Psalms 37:4

³ *Commit to the Lord whatever you do,*
and he will establish your plans.
Proverbs 16:3

¹⁰ *Whoever can be trusted with very little can also be trusted with*
much, and whoever is dishonest with very little will also be dishonest
with much. ¹¹ *So if you have not been trustworthy in handling*
worldly wealth, who will trust you with true riches?
Luke 16:10-11

¹⁸ *But remember the Lord your God, for it is he who gives you the*
ability to produce wealth, and so confirms his covenant, which he
swore to your ancestors, as it is today.
Deuteronomy 8:18

¹¹ *"For I know the plans I have for you," declares the Lord, "plans to*
prosper you and not to harm you, plans to give you hope and a
future."
Jeremiah 29:11

²⁸ *All things work together for the good of them who love the Lord and*
are called according to His purpose.
Romans 8:28

He never fails.

CHAPTER 8

'TIL DEATH DO US PART

I happen to be married to a completely amazing man and I would be telling a big story if I said our journey has been perfect. However, during the imperfect moments, we learned the power of prayer.

People still ask us if we are newlyweds because of the love and affection we give one another at all times. My husband travels a lot, so when he is away, we pray over the phone together every morning and before we lay our heads down to sleep every night. When we get on a plane together we pray before the plane takes off and if we are traveling separately, we pray via phone.

We Face-Time each other throughout the week if he is gone on tour or I am out of town. We have given ourselves a two-week limit of being away from each other. We flirt with each other all of the time, passing compliments out like they're candy and we laugh a lot at the goofiest things. We practice not sugar coating the serious things that need to be discussed and if I go 'left', he checks me firmly, but with love. We make each other accountable and we give each other respect and trust. Yes, this all took a little time and a lot of practice and we've only been married since 2012.

Just the other day, while I was working diligently on the finalities of this book, he saw how certain situations that were popping up every day concerning Amazing Testimonies and this whole process of doing an Anthology were starting to affect me. I allowed myself to get stressed out by the little "bumps in the road" to put it mildly because I was standing there looking at the finish line but every time I would take a step forward, it seemed as if someone jumped in front of me and pushed me two steps backward. In addition, I had two scripts to study, I was planning my mother's seventieth birthday celebration, having meetings for my radio show, and trying to set aside time for phone conferences and rehearsals. I was not myself and I

started to have physical issues that were similar to right before I had my stroke.

I know better and if anyone knows more than me, we have to trust God. He gave me the vision. He will give me the provision and it has to be done in His time, not mine. I gave myself deadlines because of what I wanted to do. My husband reminded me of all of these things including not being anxious for anything. When I opened the computer, he shut it down and said, "Nope, not today, you need a break. Get dressed, I'm taking you somewhere, you need a change of scenery and you need to get your mind off of this book for a little while."

Honestly, I was annoyed because all I could think about was what I needed to do to finish the book. Tony took our two, little, four legged creatures and me to the ocean for some sun and peace of mind. It was the best thing he could have done for our doggies and me. It is the 'little things' that mean the most. He could have easily gotten away from me and all my 'funk' and irritation but instead he loved me through it enough to do something about it. I forgot who I was and whose I was for a second there, but my soul-mate reminded me that I cannot allow the enemy to steal my joy. He didn't give it to me and he can't take it away. Just like I pray over this book, I pray over my marriage.

I personally cover our marriage in the Blood of Jesus daily and pray for his protection and all of our children. Collectively with his five and my two, we have seven amazing children. We enjoy working together on stage, T.V. or film. I've learned to like football so I can enjoy the games with him and almost as much as him. Our love is real and I know he prefers that I am consistent and considerate, putting him before others and giving him my best. I expect the same. My prayer is that our love will withstand the test of time and last until death do us part and beyond. Every couple has a different story and at some point, many of the couples could have chosen to end the marriage when times got too rough, but they stayed in that familiar game of love and decided to make it work. Cheers to the Champions of Love.

AMAZING TESTIMONY
by:
TONIA TYLER
Publicist
Facebook: Tonia Tyler

THE CAR ACCIDENT

In 2010, I retired from the military and I bought a BMW as a gift to myself. In 2012, I transitioned from the military and I was working as a Quality Insurance Manager and I was making really good money. At the time, my husband and I had a house. We were making great money separately with our own individual bank accounts. No joint accounts. Our marriage needed improvement and I was ready for a divorce.

We didn't have good communication or any at all and he would often tell me I couldn't tell him how to spend his money. He felt like my car was too expensive and I shouldn't have gotten it. I felt like the bulk of the bills were on me and it was frustrating. I was taking care of the kids and the house and I started to feel like I was stuck and always responsible for everything and everyone.

Others accused me of being selfish, but one day I was driving in my car listening to Katy Perry's song *Fireworks*. Those lyrics spoke to me. I cried the ugly 'boo-hoo' cry as I absorbed the words to her song. At the moment, God spoke to me, *"There's something greater for you."* I would learn later that these words were also referring to my 'Calling'. It felt like God was saying, *"Something has to change."*

I would cry several times more because I was feeling like something really did have to change. That day, I put my two-week notice in at my job. I quit my job on January 6, 2012 with no plans and I stepped out on faith knowing that I had no idea what the future held other than a retirement check from the military. I would soon find out that giving up that big fat check from my now former job would break the financial back, the

last straw. Our finances began to fall because I was the primary caretaker.

At this point, I was fed up and I didn't care if they took the house because that was an excuse for me to get out of my marriage and release my husband. I really didn't care about anything but my BMW. In 2013, the finances really fell behind, but my pride wouldn't let me stop payments on the car, which my husband was also using to get to and from work. Even though I didn't want to be married, I didn't want him to fail. He still had a job and I wasn't working.

I didn't want to make the decision to end the marriage, but in my mind if everything fell apart then it was God's way of working in His way. At the end of 2012, the house went into foreclosure and was taken in 2013. During the foreclosure my husband and I had a meeting about our finances and we sat down and went over everything that we spent. We argued off and on during the process of trying to figure out how we could survive this ordeal. In August, someone bought the house and we had thirty days to move out. We were using one car, and argued over the gas mileage daily because the price of gas was ridiculous. My BMW was the only thing we had left to argue over.

On Halloween night, it was an unusual storm so I drove very carefully and there was a strange feeling in the atmosphere. I was switching from the middle lane preparing to exit the highway and the car started swerving and hydroplaning. Then the car started to fishtail and I was facing the divider in the middle of the freeway. I knew the car wasn't going to stop and I saw that I was about to hit the brick wall. Something said, "Brace for impact." Everything was in slow motion.

I braced myself and crashed hard into the wall. My BMW was completely totaled and my airbag had deployed. When my car finally stopped, I immediately got out the car and checked myself making sure I was in one piece.

I was slightly disorientated and didn't even realize how hard it was raining for a moment. Then I reentered the car. Other passerby's stopped and came to my rescue and checked on me. A man from underneath raised his phone and said, "Do you have one of these?" I said, "Yes!" He got back in his car and took off. A woman ran over and asked if I was okay and I told her my arm was hurt from the pressure of the airbag. She assured me that the police had been called and told me to turn my car off and promised to wait until the police and paramedics came. I don't know who she was, but she was a very nice lady.

I told the police, "I saw a vision of this accident right before it happened." They said, "When you saw that you were supposed to put it out of your head." I guess that was their way of cheering me up. I told them that I was in the speed limit, in fact five miles under and no other cars were involved. The paramedics checked me and sat me in the police car while the tow truck came to take my car. I started talking to myself while calming down in the back of the police car, grateful that the police were so nice and trying to figure out what just happened and something came over me and said, "Everything will be alright."

This calm that came over me helped release my car instead of my husband and made me realize that all I had was my husband and family which was more important than all of the materialistic things I had held on to. Because of the foreclosure we were forced to work together financially and build ourselves up again. I was holding on so much to materialistic stuff that my family was suffering. Now, to this day, my husband and I get along wonderfully. All the three marriages I had, my thoughts were to run in each marriage and even though the car is what tore us apart initially, it is also responsible for bringing us together.

The answer to all my prayers happened in that car accident, no more car note, no more arguments over the amount of money we were spending on the gas. It was all taken care of. After the accident, we ended up with two cars and we had more peace and joy in our home. As the insurance company did their investigation, they deemed the car totaled and I was no longer responsible for a car note, the equity on the car covered what I owed. That night of the accident, a sense of peace came over me and I believed the feeling of peace that I had, and from that night on our finances have improved greatly and our communication got much better.

My calling manifested after that, I prayed and studied the Word more. I was able to begin helping people through my life experiences. The car accident let me know that it's time to pay attention and listen more and believe that there is more to me than I once thought. My self-worth has grown and I realize that everyone has a 'Hero Story', but not everyone hears their 'Call' and makes a step to pay attention and know they are greater

than their pain. There is a greater purpose for me to share my story so I am honored to be able to do that now. This is confirmation for me that I am on the right path. The more I listen to God's voice the more I hear Him.

Darkness cannot drive out darkness: only light can do that.
Hate cannot drive out hate: only love can do that.
-Martin Luther King Jr.

AMAZING TESTIMONY
by:
CHRISTOPHER BOOKER and LADY JASMINE BOOKER,
Official Spokesperson and Ambassador for UNITED REFUGEE
Green Counsel
Founders of BOOKER AUTISM FOUNDATION OF LEARNING
Instagram: @bookerautismfoundation

OUR STORY

Jasmine:
We've been married since 1986 in April. Chris drove all the way from Kentucky to Montgomery, Alabama and had just gotten off from work.

Chris:
I was going to go with a friend because he knew the way so we decided to make it a road trip, but he backed out at the last minute. I had very little money in my pocket and the best advice he could give me was to head south. I got on the expressway confused and someone told me to follow them, but five minutes later he took off doing 80 so he lost me. At some point, I nodded off and I was swerving in and out of lanes, but thank God, several 'passerby's blew their horns, which jolted me back into reality, but when the eighteen- wheeler truck almost ran me over, I woke up fully until I finally made it to Jasmine and immediately fell asleep. On my way back, I traveled with Jasmine in the car...

Jasmine:
We pulled over to get something to eat and before we got out of the car, Christopher told me he had to tell me something. He pulled out this beautiful velvet box and I opened it and there was a folded up piece of paper and on that paper was how much he loved me and wanted to spend the rest of his life with me.

Chris:

I was broke. Why would I invest in a ring if I didn't know if she was going to say yes or not, and Cracker Jacks stopped putting the rings in the box! We had difficult times when we got engaged. I just started College and she had just completed High School. I'll let her tell you, but I have a wonderful mother and father and even though they were divorced they were supportive.

Jasmine:

My story is a little bit different than Christopher's. My parents weren't as supportive; my mother and father were alcoholics and...

Chris:

Needless to say, we didn't get along. The compassion wasn't there and there was no love lost between her family and mine. At the time, I was about twenty-one turning twenty-two and I thought she was eighteen or nineteen, but found out that was a big lie and it made me want to walk away. Then I realized how verbally abusive her parents were to her.

Jasmine:

Well, there was that one time my mother was upset and hit me with a hot iron and to this day I have a mark on my left arm from that situation.

Chris:

From a younger age, she would tell me how they would leave her home alone for weekends to go to the Jazz Fest. She almost set the house on fire that time. The neighbors bullied her, but her parents blamed her. Her cousin's boyfriends would try to take advantage of her and she was blamed for enticing them, which was not the case. Her parents would make her buy her own food. By the time I got with her, I was infatuated. I remember taking my check and buying her food, her father would eat it up. Sometimes her father and I would argue because of that and other reasons. One day he pushed her and she almost hit her head on a marble table and her parents didn't like the idea of anyone else helping her.

Jasmine:

Another time, they kept the heat low when it was freezing outside, but my room was colder than the rest of the house. When my mother found out about my little electric heater my mom said she didn't like that. Chris took me shopping and bought me a coat that I absolutely adored.

Chris:

That coat was so ugly and she looked like somebody's granny, but it was all I could afford. Right before graduation we found out that Jasmine was pregnant and her parents said, "If you have this baby we will flush the baby in the toilet." On a brighter side, my mother paid for our wedding at the church. I didn't care much for her immediate family (her parents), but I did love her Cousin Bettie to death. Though she was Jasmine's mom's first cousin, I called her Auntie. She couldn't stand how Jasmine was being treated by her parents and when she found out Jasmine was pregnant she took her in. Bettie opened her doors to Jasmine before we married. We got along great, but unfortunately, she died of cancer. I thank God I was able to go to the hospital right before she passed.

Jasmine:

I remember her telling Chris he was like one of her sons.

Chris:

Her parents thought I was too wild and rambunctious.

Trisha:

Were you?

Chris:

That's a whole other story for another book that's never going to be made.

Jasmine:

He reminded me so much of Prince.

Chris:

No, no, no. See, that shows you how disillusioned she was. I went to Aunt Bettie's one morning to take her to school, as we were coming to an intersection, a semi-truck ran in front of us which caused me to run into a telephone pole. The car was totaled and we both were rushed to the hospital. This caused the baby to have an irregular heartbeat at the time.

I suffered a spinal injury and had to go to therapy, while Jasmine was put on bed rest. Jasmine delivered our son, Brandon, but six months later he died from heart failure. The doctors told me that I wouldn't walk again because my spine was so curved. They said I would be stricken to a wheelchair.

I didn't want to believe that so I took it into my own hands to work out and rebuild my muscles. We exhausted all our insurance and the doctors didn't want to see me so they pretty much ended other services with us. I started lifting weights and walking and exercising on my spine to sit up in a chair. It was a long painful process.

We lost our apartment and ended up staying with my brother for a week or two, then went to my father's apartment who was suffering from cancer. My father moved in with his girlfriend while we stayed, but soon came back to his place after a month or so. My father knew he was dying.

Jasmine and I then moved in with my mother for about a year and a half after Dad reclaimed his apartment. A few weeks after we moved into my mother's house, my father passed. My dad was also an alcoholic, but he was a happy alcoholic. However, I still had a problem with him drinking throughout the years, which I allowed to create a wedge between us.

I was not receptive to his parental guidance because of the alcoholism. However, close to his death we had a chance to get to know one another. I would find out that my grandmother was asked by my aunts and uncles to take my father in and her reply was, "I don't want anyone coming in my house, dying or not."

Finally, my mother told me to get my father and bring him to her house to live his final days. She said he was the only man she ever loved; he was always respectful and a gentleman, but the alcohol is what stopped us from being together. His pride and concern for dying in her house made him decline the offer. He says he loved her more than any woman, but again, the alcohol. I held my father's hand on his deathbed.

He said, "Make sure you take care of my daughters, my sister and Jasmine and my grandson." He didn't know we were having a boy. He passed while I was holding his hand. A few weeks before my father passed, we got married. Before the wedding, I sat down and talked with him and found out he was charming, funny, had a real sense of explaining things and most of all I found out that I wasted a lot of years carrying anger and bitterness. I was spiritual and hypocritical because I wasn't forgiving, but that day I forgave my dad.

Chris:

My mother has passed on and my father is still living, but I don't have any communication with him; however, I have forgiven them both. My parents smoked weed and drank so when it got crazy, my auntie would come and get me. She was a Jehovah's witness and taught me about forgiveness.

I was passed around from house to house every weekend
and I was exposed to my cousin's and aunt's boyfriend's. Three
of which tried to molest me, but I ran and told them no. I would
learn later that my grandfather, who was a Pastor, was not my
biological grandfather and he tried to sexually abuse my
mother. This may have been the reason she was an alcoholic.

I learned at a young age, that we are all born as imperfect
creatures and this is Satan's playground. We must learn to live,
laugh, and love or else life will consume you. Chris saved me
from a living hell. As a child, my closet was a safe haven for me
and my baby dolls to crawl away from the madness.

Chris:

Our second son, Jeremy, tried to commit suicide when he
was fifteen. He had a meltdown. He was crying and had a
disagreement with his girlfriend. He headed toward his desk
and picked up some scissors and he pulled them back to shove
them in the middle of his chest.

Fortunately, I was able to grab the scissors, which cut my
hand and Jasmine was able to pull the scissors out of his hand.
We took him to the Children's Hospital and the doctor tried to
pass it off as no big deal. We called our insurance company and
mentioned suing them if they didn't do something and then
they admitted him. The other doctor said he thought Jeremy
was fine and wanted to release him.

A College intern said, she had seen this behavior before and
she persuaded the hospital to keep him while she investigated
the case. She came back and mentioned autism, bi-polar and
other mental illnesses or neurological disorders that she
thought Jeremy may have had. Jeremy was born on the day
Brandon passed away February 9th at 3:45; Jeremy was born
two years later on the 9th at 4:45.

We tried to get pregnant prior to that for two years.
Jeremy's diagnosis was a learning experience. Jasmine
investigated a lot more about the spectrum of autism and how
it can be helped. For a long time, everyone told us that there
was no help. We learned you never grow out of autism, it goes
into years.

Jasmine:

I'm sitting here listening to these Doctors say, "He's going
to have a poor quality of life." I assumed by my third child
being diagnosed with autism that it was genetic. I did a lot of
investigating.

Chris:

Jeremy was very bright, with a high I.Q. Our other sons, Joshua, Jaden, and Tristan would also be diagnosed with having autism. Jeremy has a knack for electronics, technology, computers, and focuses on doing things in a productive way. His downfall was being easily persuaded into getting into things. Now, Jeremy is 26 years old with a family of his own and he is engaged to be married soon. He is doing great and very responsible with his Fiancée's daughter and two biological children. They are not all the same. Jeremy is outgoing and Jaden is shy. He's loud in the house, but not in public. Joshua is a Chameleon who will be outgoing then closes himself up in his room. Tristan is similar. Each child must be handled differently.

Jasmine:

Jaden has sensitivity to sound because he has Asperger's. I try to get people to understand the various tendencies like when they don't want to keep eye contact, those who are recluse and don't want to be alone. The kids who want to talk a lot, spin themselves or objects. You hope for a study conducted for the Fragile X Syndrome. They've been looking into it and Holly Robinson Pete mentions it, but a study for the overall development of autistic children. I have broken down in tears through all of this. I look at my eldest son, who got chased through the streets by police officers, was handcuffed and was about to be taken away from me. He was involved with a young lady who was always in trouble doing something wrong. One day he was with her and not knowing that she was shoplifting. Since he was with her and she denied her actions, he took the full blame. He was very easily persuaded which is another spectrum of autism.

Chris:

Their senses can vary, like having anger issues when something doesn't go their way. They can become harmful because they get too excited. autism is very serious and these kids are in school today being bullied because no one is aware of their condition, which in some cases leads these children to commit suicide. People don't realize that one of the spectrums of autism is OCD, schizophrenic or being in a rage. Mental retardation is a term that's outdated in the case of autism.

Many individuals are left not diagnosed properly and the lack of health insurance, lack of knowledge is the main cause. A lot of them are in prison as well. Even the elderly have autism and have never been diagnosed. There is a reason these

individuals are having meltdowns and we're not recognizing that in society. Some doctors say it's genetic and that it can skip a link or two in the line of the family.

News Media has blamed doctors and immunization shots have been accused of triggering this. Unfortunately, with all the studies, no one has come with a true factor of the spectrum of autism although their points may be valid; no one has pinpointed the true cause. What about EINSTEIN who dropped out of school, but was extremely smart? Although not confirmed, Michael Jackson who was suspected of being on the spectrum, but multi-talented. Charles Darwin, Bill Gates, and Daryl Hannah were all on the spectrum of autism and yet they were and are very accomplished. Other major celebrities actually admitted to being on the spectrum of autism publicly. These are all well-known and accomplished talented people so autism is not a bad thing and should not be looked down upon or misconstrued. Some autistic people, celebrities or not are phenomenal and brilliant and funny. Don't just rely on info you've heard, do detailed research concerning autism.

Jasmine:

One day after all of my and Chris's efforts to figure autism out and experiences with our children, I decided to seek out ways to have my own foundation. I wanted to be a helping hand to help someone else not to have to go through the trials, struggles, and tribulations. A life-long system that doesn't stop helping at the age of twenty-one. It can be overwhelming with all the doctor's visits and therapy sessions and medications, especially when you have multiple children with autism. These are humans that have to have fun in life just like you and I have to create atmospheres that suit each one of their needs.

Five years back, I came up with the name Booker autism Foundation of Louisiana. Jaden called it BAFOL at the age of seven and he said, "Isn't that the way we talk?" I adapted the acronym quickly at my smart son's suggestion and began working with an organization that was supporting my family called, AUTISM SOCIETY OF AMERICA. I got learning materials from their website, which educated me strongly. I could call and speak with a representative who would give me information. They taught us about a person's diet effecting meltdowns that triggered me into being interested in Holistic medicine. In 2013, we changed the name of the company to BOOKER AUTISM FOUNDATION OF LEARNING because we wanted to expand nationally and eventually internationally.

Autism is simply different in the way neurons in the brain communicate with each other. Visit www.bafol.org to learn more. Chris and I have been through a lot together but together is the only way we can do it.

All of the best love stories have one thing in common, you have to go against the odds to get there.

-Curiano.com

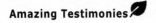
SCRIPTURES ON MARRIAGE

22 Then the Lord God made a woman from the rib he had taken out of the man, and he brought her to the man. 23 The man said, "This is now bone of my bones and flesh of my flesh; she shall be called 'woman,' for she was taken out of man." 24 That is why a man leaves his father and mother and is united to his wife, and they become one flesh.
Genesis 2:22-24

4 A wife of noble character is her husband's crown, but a disgraceful wife is like decay in his bones.
Proverbs 12:4

4 Haven't you read," he replied, "that at the beginning the Creator 'made them male and female,' 5 and said, 'For this reason a man will leave his father and mother and be united to his wife, and the two will become one flesh?' 6 So they are no longer two, but one flesh. Therefore what God has joined together, let no one separate.
Matthew 19:4-6

18 Wives, submit yourselves to your husbands, as is fitting in the Lord. 19 Husbands, love your wives and do not be harsh with them.
Colossians 3:18-19

4 Marriage should be honored by all, and the marriage bed kept pure, for God will judge the adulterer and all the sexually immoral.
Hebrews 13:4

Every setback evens the score for your comeback that guarantees a win.

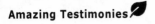

CHAPTER 9

SETBACK TO COME UP

At the end of 2000, I was pregnant with my daughter, driving down the street in a red, '87 hatchback Mazda that could have broken down at any given moment when I got the phone call that would test my faith. Actually, it was the second phone call bearing bad news. Just moments before my doctor called me with a shocker, I received a call from the apartment manager of a place that I was counting on getting because it was in walking distance of the school I had registered my five-year-old son in.

They told me it looked really good for me and apparently after I left, someone more favorable came along. "Trisha, we are so sorry, but someone came in and had the money in their hand." *Wow*, I thought, *money really does talk*. Money was also something I had very little of because I wasn't a good steward of the money I'd made earlier in the year from touring in a musical stage play. I spent thousands quickly, frivolously, and irresponsibly and now here I was pregnant, jobless, and homeless with a five-year-old.

A month and a half before I found out I was pregnant, my ex- fiancé and I mutually ended our engagement; in fact, it was one of the most beautiful break ups I had ever experienced. I walked into the room, looked at him, and said, "What are we doing? You're not happy and I'm miserable."

"It's been a wonderful journey Trisha Mann," he responded. We hugged, kissed, I told a joke, and we laughed and talked about what's next. Little did I know that the end was just the beginning and what had ended sweet would soon turn sour.

I had no idea that a month and a half later I would have a doctor tell me I was three and a half months pregnant. Just weeks before that news came, my son walked up to me in the bathroom of my friend Chris's apartment and said very boldly, uttering his first prophecy as he put his hand on my stomach, "You've got my little sister in there Mommy." "Boy," I said,

"Stop playing! Mommy is not having a little sister any time soon!"

It turned out that my son knew more than me and that would be his first prophetic message. My Bestie Chris was kind enough to let us sleep on his floor in the living room of his tiny one bedroom apartment. I had been living with my ex-fiancé, but after the break- up, I moved out. A friend of mine, named April, who was very intuitive was on the phone with me all the way in Chicago. She said, "Trisha, I keep seeing a baby around you. Are you pregnant?" I said, "Girl please, I'm sure that if I was I would have known by now, but no I'm not pregnant."

One night I went to Bible study and the pastor whom everyone addressed as Prophet Manny said loudly, "Sister Trisha! I keep seeing a little girl wrapped around your leg." I looked down at my leg and thought to myself, *Either it's me or everyone around me is on Crack because I'm not pregnant! I have not had sex since my break-up and he was the only person I was with the entire time we were engaged, so what is really going on?*

After that, I had another conversation with April saying, "I think you need to take a pregnancy test and get checked out." I laughed it all off at first because I was still having a period on time. However, between her mentioning it at least three times, my bible study pastor telling me he saw a little girl wrapped around my leg and my son being so emphatic, I finally bought a pregnancy test just to prove everyone wrong, but I ended up being the one proven wrong when the results came back positive.

All kinds of thoughts went through my head and by the reaction of everyone else around me, no one seemed happy about the news. A woman named Mary talked to me about the importance of making the right decision where my unborn baby was concerned. She prayed with me and assured me that no matter what my situation looked like, God was in control, and this baby was meant to be here. I mentioned abortion to her and she told me that it was not my decision to make.

I went to the doctor and saw my child at three and a half months growing inside of me. At first I didn't believe him when he said I was fourteen and a half weeks pregnant, but something came over me when I saw the sonogram. I thought about Mary and all the people who saw my child before I knew I was even pregnant. Then the dreams and visions of her that I had myself came back to me. I saw this little girl several times

in a dream the same way I saw my son before he was born and I had a vision about him before I knew I was pregnant with him.

That vision was crystal clear almost as if I were awake. My deceased grandmother and deceased Uncle Robby walked through the door looked at me and said, "You are pregnant, you're going to have a little boy, and he's going to be very special. Whatever you do, don't get an abortion." Now the reality of having another child out of wedlock, the thought of telling my ex who had already moved on and was back with his ex on top of my present situation and what about my career? The dreams of being an actress were flying out of the window. My mother was so disgusted with me and disappointed in me that she sounded like she didn't want to talk to me.

One night, my pager went off and it was a message from my ex who had obviously been influenced by outsiders who didn't know my heart, my spirit, or me. It had been a month since we spoke and he said, "You haven't heard from me and you won't hear from me until there's a baby, if there's a baby." My heart sank at the sound of those cold words coming from someone who had earlier in the year gotten on stage in front of thousands in my hometown and proclaimed his love for me saying, "Thank you Chicago for giving me my wife, Trisha Mann." *Why would I lie about such a thing and don't you know the kind of person I am?* Is what I was thinking.

It wasn't long after that moment that I felt depression setting in and I began to ponder thoughts of suicide daily. It got to the point that I actually started to envision how I would do it, if I would leave a note behind and how I could make sure that my sister or mother would take care of my son. I thought I had it all figured out and I was gaining the courage to not only take myself out of the game, but to also take out this unborn baby, that no one but me seemed to want, growing inside of me. One night, I woke up suddenly to the feeling of two hands grabbing my thighs and thrusting me downward. My legs were pushed apart forcefully and I felt a hand reaching inside of me. I looked down in between my legs expecting to see an intruder who was trying to rape me, but no one was there. It took me a second to realize that I was having a demonic attack and whatever it was, this thing was trying to get to my baby. I started calling on Jesus, but was instantly muted and paralyzed. I looked over at my son who was sleeping peacefully and tried to call out to my friend Chris who was in the other room, but nothing came out. I continued to think about Jesus and the

169

entity continued to torment me. It seemed to become frustrated that it couldn't reach my baby. Finally, it left me alone and I was exhausted from what seemed to be a fight for my life and the baby's.

I've experienced enough supernatural episodes in my life since I was a child, but never had I called on Jesus and the warring angels didn't show up on my behalf. I expect anyone reading this that has never seen, heard, or felt something spiritual would think I am out of my mind and that is completely understandable. However, for those who know exactly what I'm talking about, never give up on calling on the Name of Jesus no matter what spiritual battle you're in.

The next morning, the Lord spoke to me and said, *"You have two choices. You can choose Satan or you can choose Me."* God allowed me to be tormented that night without Him coming to my aid to let me know that if I chose to commit suicide and take myself and my innocent seed out of the equation of Life, what I dealt with the night before was just a taste of what I would deal with for eternity. I chose God.

I immediately fell on my face and repented for my thoughts and I prayed to God to help me and give me the strength to make it through this pregnancy. I desired to be closer to God, so I took Mary's advice and changed the music in my car to Fred Hammond, Yolanda Adams, Donnie McClurkin and as many Gospel Artists I could jam to and get my praise and worship on to while I drove around trying to find a place for my son and this new baby to be. I had no idea how I would pay for it, but I knew that God knew more than me and He was going to make a way.

After receiving the phone call about the people giving the apartment that I desired to someone else, I immediately received another call. The minute I hung up disappointed from that first phone call, the phone rang again and this time it was my doctor. "Ms. Mann, I'm sorry to inform you, but our test results show that your baby is going to be born with heart problems, kidney problems, and Down-Syndrome. If you would like for me to authorize a legal abortion, I can do that, but we need to do it quickly."

Prior to this call, I was forced to have an amniocentesis for DNA proof for my ex so he could see for sure that our baby girl was his since we had been broken up for a short while. These types of tests have been known to result in the death of the fetus, but I didn't know that until after it was done. I was

happy to do it because I knew she was his and I wanted him to have peace of mind from all the 'talking heads' of doubt in his ear.

The minute the doctor said his last words to me about my daughter having Down syndrome, I instantly with no hesitation responded, "I rebuke that in the Name of Jesus Dr._and my daughter is going to be born perfectly healthy. If you have any good news for me in the future, please call me anytime, however, I don't want to hear anything else negative about my baby. Thank you."

Needless to say, he was really angry with me and hung up the phone with a tone of irritation. I had absolutely no fear of what he said and I simply did not accept it. When I got back to Chris's place, he looked at me and said, "I have to move back to Chicago and I have two weeks to be out of here my friend, so you've got to find somewhere else to go." I made many phone calls in that two week period, trying to find another floor or hopefully couch to sleep on and most of those calls ended with, "Trisha, I'm so sorry, I'll be praying for you or I'll keep an ear to the ground for you."

The two weeks was almost up and doubt was trying to slip in my thoughts again. Finally, a fellow actress friend of mine, Gloria said, "I have a tiny storage room filled with boxes and a small day bed you and your son can sleep on." I moved in and every morning I got up, took my son to kindergarten, and searched for an apartment on faith because all I had was four hundred dollars in my bank account. Most of the money was going toward application fees, food and gas for my little red 'Go-Cart,' but something in me just wouldn't give up and I was determined that my baby girl was going to have a roof over her head by the time she entered this world.

Gloria used to make these amazing Gospel music cassette tapes for me to listen to in the car and we talked about God and prayed together a lot. When you're going through a storm, it's best to be surrounded by those who will lift you up and encourage you, not those who tear you down and add insult to injury. One day after looking for a job and a place, I got to Gloria's house exhausted and received a call from a former boyfriend's ex-girlfriend. Sounds like something straight out of a soap opera, right?

Desiree said, "Trisha, I know this sounds strange, but God spoke to me and told me to give you something and I have to be obedient. Where are you? I need to come give this to you now."

171

I was surprised and curious and after getting the 'okay' from Gloria to give out her address, I waited for Desiree to come by. When she arrived, she handed me a check and said, "I really had to question God on this because I wasn't sure about this amount, but I knew I had to be obedient."

We really didn't know each other that well, but she and I went to the same church and I heard nothing but good things about her. She handed me a check for five hundred dollars, gave me a hug, and left just as quickly as she came. I was stunned and extremely thankful that I now had nine hundred dollars toward the new place that I believed was a blessing from God.

The next day, my mother called and said that a friend of hers, Carlan, of whom I hadn't seen since childhood called her and was led to give me a thousand dollars. I was in disbelief yet so grateful. Not too long after that, I received a call from an apartment near my son's school in which he would have been starting soon. They congratulated me on being approved for my new place, but they needed $2,000 total for first and last month's rent. I told them that I was $100 short and they said, "No problem, we can put it on the next month's rent."

Less than a month after moving into my new place I gave birth to a beautiful baby girl, Dena, named after my dear sister-friend from High school. She was born a month early and the doctors said that she was the healthiest premature baby they had seen in a long time. She had no Down-Syndrome, no kidney problems, and no heart problems, but she had one of the most beautiful smiles. That baby girl is now in High School, taller than me and a very talented Fashion Designer, Model, Basketball and Volleyball player.

I had no idea how I would pay that next month's rent, but her father helped me over the first hump that month and my Heavenly Father allowed me the ability to live in that place with my two amazing children for the next five years, continue to pursue my career and successfully elevate in it and then it was time for a new chapter to begin.

I am grateful that Dena and her dad have an amazing relationship, which was my main desire from day one. He is a wonderful dad and we have a great co-parenting friendship. I often tell women who are struggling with separations, break-ups, or divorces that their main focus should be the children and not your emotions about a relationship that is over. Never use the child as a pawn to get back at the other parent and

never stop them from being in the other parents' life because you're angry at the outcome or something he did in the relationship. That type of behavior will only hurt the child.

I was and will forever more be grateful to Gloria and Chris for blessing me with a place to lay my head. I will always be thankful to Mary for talking some sense into me and making me realize, if that child wasn't meant to be, she would never have been conceived. I will also be grateful to Desiree and Carlan for being obedient to the voice of the Holy Spirit and blessing me out of the blue financially. I am truly grateful to my daughter's father for not listening to the naysayers or even his own thoughts at that time and I'm thankful that he has been a wonderful part of his daughter's life from the day she was born. I have learned through the years that no matter how unorthodox something may seem, when that still small voice speaks to us to do an act of kindness, we should listen. We just may be the catalyst in helping someone who has been setback to come up. To God be the Glory! He is so AMAZING!

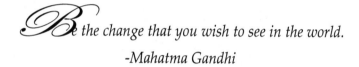

Be the change that you wish to see in the world.
-Mahatma Gandhi

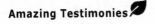

AMAZING TESTIMONY
by:
CHARLES CLARK
Transformation Speaker
Honorary Doctor of Divinity
www.cclarkinspire.com

GANGBANGER TO LIFE CHANGER

I lost my father, who was in the Special Forces of the Army, at the age of six in a fatal car accident about five minutes from home. Someone ran him off the road and to this day everyone thinks it was foul play. My dad was a very handsome, tall, charming man with a bad boy edge. He was not only in the military, but he knew martial arts.

His truck went through a woman's yard, flipped over a few times and my father hit a tree stump that caught the front axle of his truck and caused it to flip over four or five times. He was thrown out of the truck into the cornfields. Unfortunately, he wasn't wearing a seatbelt. He fought for his life because the paramedics could see that he crawled from the spot he got thrown from toward the woman's house.

I had just seen my father alive a few hours before this. He was going to a celebration his boss was having for him along with other co-workers, because he'd gotten promoted to a high position at his job. He and my mom had just gotten engaged. When he went to leave, she ran out to stop him and said, "Don't go, please stay here. Something's not right; I don't want you to go." They went back and forth for five minutes discussing why he shouldn't go, but he decided to go.

I was sitting in the front seat buckled up ready to go with him because I was my dad's road dog. I went everywhere with him. My mother said, "If you go you can't take my son." He gave me a kiss on my forehead, mom took me out of the car, and Dad said, "We are going fishing when I get back." He stopped in the middle of the road and looked back at me because I was crying and he said, "I love you booby."

175

I kept waiting for dad to come home that night and I kept asking mom when was he coming home. My dad was very punctual because he was a military man. His cousins and lots of other family members came to the house around a quarter to midnight and got me. My dad's favorite cousin and his wife Barbara Ann woke me up and she looked at me with swollen eyes, it was obvious that she had been crying, she said, "Everything is going to be okay, we gotta' go see your Daddy." I knew even at that age that something was wrong.

They took me to the woman's house. I was sitting in the car, but I had to use the bathroom by the well. While I was using the bathroom, I remember seeing the cornfield move. To this day I think that that was my father's last crawl because my cousins Kenneth and Louis found him in the cornfield right after that. I saw them pick my dad up off the ground and they tried to cover my eyes up.

I was so hurt and crushed and my mother took it hard to the point she lost a lot of weight and she was depressed. I had to become a man early. From the age of six until the age of twelve I had a lot of anger in me. I felt empty, so I started training in the martial arts like my dad and I played baseball and football and every time other boys on the teams would have their father's there to support them, a rage built in me.

I started to sneak out in the streets; hanging with the pimps and drug dealers. I became a Street Enforcer which meant I was someone who would potentially hurt anyone who owed a debt to the pimps and drug dealers. They knew I was missing having a father in my life so they took advantage of that by loving on me like a dad would and I fell for the 'Ok-e-doke' becoming a puppet for the devil. During my mid-teens and on into adulthood, I was involved in shootings and I witnessed more deaths than you see in a gangsta' hood movie. I saw many close friends die.

From the ages of sixteen to twenty-one can be considered as my main course of becoming and being evil. I remember saying I wanted to be the baddest 'MF' around. I felt like it was part of my destiny. I was spiritually dead and I didn't care about nothing. I woke up laughing at the fact that I was still alive because I was such an evil person. I would break people's bones that owed less than ten dollars. I was involved in shootouts and was forced to watch several executions. All the hurt in me went overboard onto others.

One time I busted a man's window, pulled him out the car and shoved a 45. Caliber gun in his mouth and pulled the trigger, but the gun did not go off, so I beat him half to death. He survived, but I rearranged his face. I stabbed several people. One was setting up to rob me so I waited for him. I'm very good with a blade. If I didn't kill you it's because I didn't intend to. I wanted people to remember me. I saw him first and stabbed him in his arms, upper chest, leg, and hip areas. I wanted him to always be reminded of the pain.

The Martial Arts taught me the places on a person's body to stab. There were more serious situations that I won't go into detail with. I protected the prostitutes and I called myself the 'Insurance Man'. I was heavy in selling drugs and I got set up by some people I was dealing with. One day, I was about to make the biggest drop of my career; then I got busted. I received ten years and six months for my crime; however, I only did seven years and five months in a federal penitentiary.

Once you get called for prison, you have to wait. That wait was stressful. I started losing my hair and my weight and I was hoping to get called and get this sentence over with. When I stepped onto the prison yard, I felt weak and powerless. Everyone was looking at me like, "Who is this guy, what is he in for?" I was walking to the laundry room when it hit me, *I'm about to spend my golden years in prison.*

I felt like I let my mom down and the spirit of my father, even my grandmother. I started finding my hustle by opening up a store in prison. My first three and a half years I didn't get it and people knew who I ran with. When they found out who I ran with, I got automatic respect. They knew I wasn't a snitch. I was cool. I joined the weight lifting squad and the football team and became MVP, but in prison you will always be tested. I got tested about three times.

My second month, I decided to use the phone and I called my Grandma first, then I called my mom. This guy had the phone; he was arguing and cussing at his girl. He stood there after she hung up. I said, "Can I use the phone?" He said, "Get it like Grant got Richmond." I said, "Man, give me the phone." He said, "You punk, *blank* Al B. Sure yellow nigga, after I beat you with this phone, I'm going to stick this phone..." I wrapped the phone around his neck and beat the brakes off of him. He requested to go to another section after that.

Going into my fourth year, a new breeze came in. I was by a microwave making pizza with tortilla chips. This guy lost his mom and sister and he couldn't go to the funeral. He was ready to self- destruct. I don't know what happened, but God said, *"This is the beginning of what you're supposed to be."* I said, "Brother look, I don't know your name, but your mom and sister, it was their time." I told him what I had been through and I felt the Holy Spirit start to come alive in me.

I knew at that moment that something was happening. The prisoner who was the assistant to the Chaplain said, "You need to come in and speak." I said, "Nah, I'm not a speaker, I just had a moment." While lying down, I had a dream about my daddy. He said, "I knew I was going to die and it was my time to leave so that you could do what you're called to do." He said, "You've been in prison since I've been gone and this time when I kiss you on your fore-head which was his way of protecting me, I will release everything from you."

I woke up and felt empty in a good way. I started speaking to people in the Chapel and CEO's came to me asking for advice. The Assistant warden would ask me for advice too. I knew this is what I should do. "God, if I try to be this next big speaker, people will mock me and take me for a joke because of my past experience." I said, "I will have a red flag," and God said, *"What color is my Son's blood? Do not live by other people's opinions but live by My truth and you will be okay."*

I was released from prison and went to a re-entry program. I stayed current with technology so I wouldn't be confused when I got out into the world. I got into acting, something I would do with my prison buddies. They said I should act. I thought it wasn't my thing, but found out it was. I had money put away when I got out in 2009 so that I wouldn't be completely broke and stayed with my aunt whose son was in the streets doing bad things. I mentored him for a year and he got better. I landed my first film in 2010; I did modeling and a web series.

There were times I was struggling financially and looking for a decent job. I was spending and the funds were depleting and I didn't like that. My daughter was to be born soon and I got tired of working several jobs. I went back to my old stomping grounds and my flesh was yearning to get back into the 'hustle' so I could make some real money. God spoke to me and said, *"I didn't bring you this far for nothing, for you to bring back My glory null and void. This is your last chance."*

I felt a spiritual consciousness. I remembered the first week of being home, I had a dream, and I saw myself in a casket. I started crying from conviction. I was once a street enforcer, gangbanger and drug dealer and now I'm a two time IRSA (Internet Radio Star Awards) award winner, I'm a contest winner for Devon Franklin's AT&T Inspired Mobility Contest and I'm also a grand prizewinner of the AT&T 28 Days Moments that Matter.

Also, under the prestigious Dr. Yomi Garnett who inducted me into the Hall of Fame in the Institute of the Global Human Excellence, I recently won the Men Of Vision's, I Am a Testimony Award. I just received my Honorary Doctorate of Divinity. Five years from now, I see myself maturing in my leadership and growing greater in my purpose and my anointing in God so I can be fully increased through His Glory. My advice to others is, every struggle has a victory; it's not the struggle itself, but the physical endurance to get through it. Life doesn't end when you make mistakes, but life begins when you learn from them.

Your life does not get better by chance, it gets better by change.

- Jim Rohn

AMAZING TESTIMONY
by:
BERNA BLU
Singer/Entertainer/Musician
Bernablu.net

TROUBLED

I believe I was twenty-two when I was diagnosed with mental illness. In 2007, I went into a nervous breakdown and got diagnosed. It was a series of stressful situations for any normal person. I had just left my daughter's father who was physically, sexually, and mentally abusive. He said, "Put your dreams aside because there are too many men involved in the industry. Pick your family or your dreams or we will split up." I picked my family because that was the only thing that I never had. Family meant way more than my purpose. I wanted that more than my dreams because I was abandoned from birth. My mom was abusing drugs and my grandmother and stepfather at the time took me from her. She was physically abusive to men because she was abused by her father. Grandmother was being beat with brooms by her mom and her dad was cheating and they divorced because she was abused my mother's father.

On one of his drunken occasions, my mother's father raped her. She got into gangs at twelve and she got pregnant with me at fifteen. My grandmother was married twice. Grandma married a white man who was her third or fourth husband. He hated my mother and uncle. He called them niggers and to this day calls me a nigger.

My uncle and mom got kicked out of the house at twelve. My grandfather gave my grandmother an option to choose because they had started to rebel. He told her to send them away. My grandmother packed their bags and they left, got in the streets and got in trouble. They had their addictions. My addiction needed a man's love. You choose bad things, you have bad experiences. I was sixteen when I got pregnant and we reaped from our mistakes.

I kept crying out to God and the only reason I'm here on consequences earth now is because of God. I went down a wrong path. Along comes this guy who drinks alcohol, had piercings, the girls wanted him, and he had tattoos all over. We were twenty-one when he introduced me to alcohol. He dragged me to his hell but thank God our kids have hearts of gold. Soon after, I got a call that my grandmother who was always a consistent provider, had cancer.

I left my ex and got an apartment. I told him, "we have a baby and we can't live with your mom anymore, we're parents and I want to raise my kids the way I want to and that's your ultimatum." He declined and wanted to stay with his mom, so I left him. Since I was six years old, I had been molested, abused, and beaten by my grandparents for no apparent reason. My grandmother once cut my eye and threw a shoe at me.

I told the teacher the reason my eye was cut and the school called my grandmother and told her what I'd said. She picked me up, took me to the house, grabbed my sister and patted her on the head and said, "Look, this is my daughter. You will never be my daughter you got thrown on me because nobody wanted you." I thought I had let go of that memory, but I never did. I thought that if I didn't talk about the things that happened to me they would go away.

My neighbors invited me to church when I was six and the lady was really nice to me, she was filled with God but she died of cancer early. She was a blessing on earth. She deserved to live longer than seventy, but she was taking care of everyone else. My neighbors are the reason I had God in my life. The wife was the reason her husband went to church every Sunday and he was the very man that molested me at six years old.

I would be dancing and it was sick and twisted, but I would put on the husband's hats and her costume jewelry and dresses. They would sit on the couch and I would entertain them. They put on Meryl Haggard and I would dance. If she would leave the room, he would say, "Come here, and give me a kiss."

I would go to kiss him on the cheek and he would make me kiss him on the lips and say, "No, like the movies, use your tongue." He would kiss me on my neck and stick his hand in my privates. He was the same man who baptized me at my church and I prayed that one day his own guilt would convict his spirit. I wanted him to see my pain.

His wife, however, was the only one who didn't do mean things to me. My grandparent's let me spend the night over

181

their house. She sang songs with me and read the Bible and stayed with me until I fell asleep. Her daughter was hooked on drugs as a teen so she took me in like a daughter because she didn't have a relationship with her own. I enjoyed going to church because it was the only place that didn't judge me.

My own family would judge me when I sang so I sang in the closet at home. I accepted God, but I thought I could lose Him. I often got angry about my past, because I had been slapped in the face, had television's thrown at me, had my eyes cut up, and eventually dropped off with my mom who was at the drug dealers house and I remember her having sex with him while I was in the bed with her and I was awake. I was six and didn't want to say anything and get in trouble. By the time I was older, because I had a 'religious trip', they had all this textbook information of what was wrong with me saying I was mentally ill and I had a breakdown from lack of sleep. Soon I started to record songs after leaving my baby's dad. I got good feelings when I sang and I worked full time and went to record after work, so I had no sleep.

The news of my grandmother dying didn't help either. My intentions and everything I demonstrate are good, but I was locked into solitude and institution. She called and told me, "I've got cancer and I'm leaving to Lofton." I was left with my mom. At the end of all of that, my kids are a representation of a cycle change. People call me cocky, but I stand for something really big and powerful. I am turning thirty and I don't have time for people questioning me.

I've been sick since August 2015 and things have been overlooked for a year. I just got diagnosed with a bacteria disease that can only be cured through antibiotics. They passed it off as something else. I've chosen to not take medication for my mental illness. These are the same meds that made me suicidal. I was like a zombie, a walking vegetable.

There was an occurrence in which I put my hands on my sister at my daughter's birthday party. My sister is someone who has poked at me for thirty years; she doesn't believe in God and was now poking at me again at my daughter's party. She grabbed me by my hair and I hit her in the face, but everyone that saw this was saying, "Mentally ill Bernadette hit her poor sister." They didn't see what she was doing. My daughter had no clue what happened.

I oversee foster girls who went through the same thing I went through and my sister wanted me to put them out. My creativity keeps me up and stress keeps me awake. That is another reason for my lack of sleep. The mental health system is abusing meds and killing people with it. I am going to give of myself by helping other children going through what I experienced, but everyone sees me as the pretty girl with a little bit of talent and a little bit of brains who wants to be famous.

I don't care about fame. I never once laid down to a dream. My dream is the truth and sharing my gift. I've been doing it my way and my way hasn't worked, but I told God to please send me an Angel. I allowed things to sidetrack me because the devil blocks things. Relationship-wise, I didn't have healthy love; love has been a drug for me. Love on earth from humans became priority over God's love. I've felt things I couldn't explain, tingles in my arm and chills in my body. I can recall my church closed their doors one day without any warning. At the time, I was a seventeen year old youth group leader for the music department and one day they just came and told me that the church was closing down. No warning, I knew nothing.

One night I sang at church. One person out of 6,000 of my Facebook fans had an offer from me to pick them up and give them a ride to church. I helped this one guy who was homeless with no friends, family, or food and when he got a place, someone broke in and robbed him. He thought someone gave him something; they slipped him some drugs. A prophet spoke to me and he gave me confirmation. "God's going to bless you, something in your life is going to shake everything up and bring your family back together again, say FLOW!" I put a hash tag of FLOW on my Facebook page to encourage everyone.

I recently went to Ohio and was performing on stage with a Blues Legend, Crazy Marvin, who embraced me and took me under his wing like I was his own daughter. It was like a dream come true, the way my Godmother would have expected my life to be. I never got closure, by saying goodbye to her because she had Lymphoma Cancer and then she was gone. She was given seven years to live, but she only lived three of those years. It was a shock to me and I wasn't able to sing at the funeral. For the last three years, I have been crying in my heart wishing I had spent more time with her. She always told me, "Only God knows your heart." I believe she said this because many people don't understand me as a person, but I've always had a strength in me, no matter what the world brings me, I always come out stronger because of my faith in God. At the end of the day I keep coping and believing.

I have been counseling foster children at the Vision group home who have experienced various traumatic experiences. I got hired on as a music therapist and certified counselor and my job was to bring music into the home as a source of counseling. The music made the girls happier and my happy, energetic spirit helped. It was a foster home with five girls between the ages of five and fifteen and I fell in love with them. They became like my second children. I have bigger goals of working with larger groups of children to make more of an impact, but this small group has made a difference in my life. I can relate to each one of these girls because of all that I've been through. I took them dancing, to resorts on mountains and I brought instruments for them to learn to play. I brought them to my house and reenacted Fashion Runway. We made a music video together. I took great care with how they looked up to me. They will be fine with the right mentors planting the proper seeds inside of them. They are beautiful and I know that their lives will prosper and one day they will have stories to tell and others to mentor to.

There is always light at the end of the tunnel for people with mental health issues. Often times it seems like there's no way out. Mental illness can be a dark experience, but it doesn't have to be. It can consume a person's body, mind, and soul, but it doesn't have to. I have had to conquer and succeed while accepting that I am bi-polar, but I also accept that I can live a healthy and fulfilling life and I know that it doesn't have to end in suicide. There is light at the end of the tunnel. Albert Einstein and many famous people have had mental illness. God is the only reason I am living today and He has always pulled me out of any darkness. Mental illness doesn't mean that I am less of a person it just means that I have to try a little harder.

AMAZING TESTIMONY
by:
AMBER ESTES-SPEESE
Author of Wolves In Sheep Clothing
favored2bless58@gmail.com

WICKED CULT

I was a freshman in College, and although I was involved in church and the Black Choir, I was seeking more spiritually and no one could give me the answers I needed. I went on semester break in December of 1983, and when I got back home to Chicago, I asked my best friend about going partying. Instead, she told me about a church in Chicago she wanted me to visit. She invited me to this small storefront church and when I got there, the women had no makeup or jewelry on and they were really homely looking. The men looked fine though. I did feel the presence of God and I didn't understand it then, but I felt God.

The Pastor, who had five children with his wife, the first lady of the church, who he ended up putting out later and marrying my Bible study teacher, reminded me of my father and was very charismatic and in his late thirties. He was a former gangbanger, cocaine user, and pimp who had other children as well. He asked me if I was born again, I said, "Yes, I think so, I go to church, and I'm in the choir." He said, "That doesn't save you."

He took me through the Sinners prayer on Christmas day as I sat in the back of his car and then he dropped my friend and I off at my mother's house. I used to feel emptiness and a void on the inside of me, like something was missing even though I went to the campus church and was in the choir. I would pray in the morning and at night and was reading my word, but it wasn't until I did the Sinner's prayer with this Pastor that I felt later that evening that I didn't feel that void I once had. I figured out that I had truly accepted Jesus Christ, as my Lord and Savior.

I went back to school after Christmas break and I actually had an audible experience with God. I was wrestling back and forth with God because I was very popular on Campus, dating the captain of the defense on the football team and I was also a Kappa Sweetheart. I was battling with the thoughts that it didn't take all that to be saved.

I lived on the twelfth floor of my dorm. One day I heard God audibly tell me to walk up the entire twelve flights of stairs. I was obedient. It was hard and I was getting tired. I didn't know many scriptures so I was surprised to hear the scripture, "You can do all things through Christ who strengthens you." (Philippians 4:13) When I got to the twelfth floor and put my key in to unlock the door, another scripture came to me, "Well done my good and faithful servant, enter into the joy of your Lord." (Matthew 25:21) Again I didn't remember scripture like that, so I knew it was God speaking to me.

I got in my room, packed up all of my jeans and anything tight and provocative, gave it away and I began to look homely. I was going to the campus Bible study to be a witness for the Lord. People would come to Bible study just to see what happened to me. We had a group on campus made up of mostly women and we would go home to Chicago to that pastor's church that my best friend took me to.

About nine to ten of us would leave on Friday and return late Sunday. A year after I joined the church, we were told we could only go to work, school, and church. No movies, no sports, or any other activities were allowed. We were cut off from family members and friends who didn't get saved or think the way we did about salvation, with the 'Hell Fire and Brimstone teachings.' Everyone at the church was between their twenties and early thirties. We couldn't even fellowship with those who didn't go to our church or to our church affiliate.

I had been sensing something was wrong with this church and its methods, but the pastor taught us to obey them who are ruling over us. He was misquoting the Word and pimping us. We were young people who really had a heart for God and would get on the El trains and minister to people and actually save them. He always used the Word to control us. "Hebrews 13:17" he would quote, "Obey them who have rule over you."

It started getting really crazy when we were forced to give our whole paycheck to the pastor. I lived off of one check for the month and things got very tight. Other church members

went completely broke and were not able to live off of just one check. We had to sale bricks for the church which was promised would have the names of the patrons who purchased the bricks from us on it once the new church was built.

I remember being in the pastor's office during church service one day and he scratched my palm underneath with his middle finger. I said, "Why are you doing that? That didn't feel comfortable." He said if any man does this, he wants to have sex with you. I said, "No man would ever do that because it's a sin." I was never promiscuous and had been celibate for four years up until this point.

He asked me to meet him to drop something off at his mother's home where he had an office in his mom's basement. We got in his van and I said, "Why are we in the van?" It was then that I was violated and molested by my pastor in the back of his van. I felt paralyzed with fear as he raped me and I knew it wasn't right. During the act I cried and I kept telling him, "This is not right, this is not right." When it was over he said, "You can't tell anyone about this. You can go now." Just like that. I cried all the way home and felt very nasty. I took a shower and kept questioning God and trying to wash the sin off of me, "How God, how can this be? Am I going to hell?" Whenever I went to church after that, I felt shame and I couldn't pray. I wasn't active with praise and worship because it was hard to sing and be joyful. Then it happened again, once at his mother's home. I was doing administrative work for him and he threatened me to be sexual with him. He physically forced me more aggressively this time. Then, the final time it happened at a hotel where he told me to meet him. After that I couldn't take it anymore. The sad part is that I wasn't the only one he did this to in the church. There were at least six other women who had the courage to tell and some of the women in the church got pregnant and were forced to have abortions.

That happened in 1987 and it devastated me. To be violated like that was like being caught up in a web of lies, confusion, and deceit. We couldn't even watch TV, unless it was religious so I would keep my radio station on a Christian channel at all times. One day I was listening to WYCA and I heard Pastor John Eckhardt come on the air, "Wake up, wake up, wake up!' On this particular day he was teaching on the difference between worshipping a leader and obeying a leader.

Before my pastor violated me, I told him that I thought we were all idolizing him, but he continued to use scripture to manipulate my thoughts. We were serving God under a lot of fear because we were taught condemnation and not conviction. Apostle John Eckhardt said at the end of his radio program, "Write in for questions or comments," and he prayed from Win Worley's book called Spiritual Warfare Prayers. I wrote in and asked him what was the difference between worshipping a pastor and obeying a pastor?

He sent me that prayer book with a sticky note telling me to call him. I was afraid to call him because we couldn't talk to anyone outside of our church. After the hotel visit with my pastor, I was ready to call and when I did, I asked Pastor Eckhardt about pierced ears and spirits since we weren't allowed to pierce our ears. I can't remember his response, but he must have discerned spiritually that I was under a controlling leadership.

I told him we weren't supposed to talk to anyone outside our church and he said that's a lot of control for a Pastor to stop his congregation from talking to people. He asked me to visit his church and I told him we were not allowed to visit other churches. I said, "We have church every day except Monday." He said, "Monday is our deliverance day," I said, "Let me pray about it," and he gave me the address and said, "When you come, let me pray with you." I decided to go, but I couldn't go alone. I took my aunt with me and when we got to Pastor Eckhardt's church, the women didn't have any doylies on their heads and some women had pants on. I thought to myself, *Oh no, these people aren't saved*. The devil was telling me that I needed to leave.

I sat in the back and kept looking back at the door as I experienced constant torment. I was going back and forth filled with confusion and fear. I have grown to learn that the battlefield is always in the mind. I told my aunt, "Let's go because I don't think we're in the right place anyway", since I didn't see or hear Pastor Eckhardt. When we got up to go, I heard Eckhardt's voice say, "Hello saints, let's praise Him!"

I felt an instant release and then he said, "Come on down, it's time for deliverance!" When I went down for the deliverance ministry, there was a young lady, I believe his niece, and she was receiving people for prayer. I told her, "I'm not trying to be funny, but Pastor Eckhardt told me he wants to pray for me specifically." She got Pastor Eckhardt and his words to me were, "Sister, you need to leave from that church,

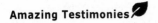

he has too much control. I have my own service at 2:00 p.m. and we go to Joliet."

My deliverance process started that night and it wasn't until that next Sunday when we went to our visiting church and a pastor said, "Many of you have been in Egypt and when you walk completely around that altar you will have full deliverance." I was completely delivered and I never stepped foot in that other church again.

I was definitely in a cult, there was witchcraft and control going on and I thank God that I was successfully delivered. To this day I am free of that bondage. John 8:36 says, *"If the Son set you free you are free indeed."* If anyone reading this is in a situation like this or knows someone who is, know that God can and will deliver you or your loved one out of this and your misery and mess will become your message to set others free. God is faithful. If you want to change anything, feel free.

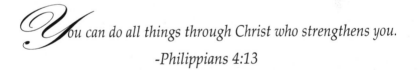

You can do all things through Christ who strengthens you.

-Philippians 4:13

AMAZING TESTIMONY
by:
KAREN DELL
"Mother Goose"
Wife, writer and mother to all the feathered friends who live in
BALBOA LAKE, especially "Calvin aka Legacy"

THE DEVIL HAD ME

I was just like anyone else. I was out there lost, looking for God anyway I could. I was always very sensitive, before my family left to move from Iowa, I was repairing from Osteomyelitis. My grandpa died and my dad wanted to leave, he was an only child and it was too painful for him. He said, "Let's go to California, let's move," so we moved down to the Cosa Mesa area down by Newport Beach and I didn't fit in ya' know, I was this tender hearted little girl whose last name was Rash. Everyone would tease me by saying, "Hey Butt rash, diaper rash" and I thought, *How fun is that, let's just tease this little pale, skinny, tall girl.* I'd cry and my mom would say, "Turn the other cheek, turn the other cheek," and well, they'd smash that one, too.

I would say to God, "Why are these kids so mean to me? What have I done to them?" I didn't understand and I couldn't comprehend it. One day, my mom said, "You know you really don't have to take that" and I guess I just got angry. Something snapped and if you've ever seen that movie, ME, MYSELF, AND IRENE, I was so sweet and kind and I couldn't hurt anybody but these kids, they just wanted to beat up on me and I didn't know what to do with that so I got to the point of, I was going to do a Sonny and Muhammad Ali fight.

If somebody was going to throw the ball, I was going to knock them down right there and that's it. I had that in me where, *nobody's gonna hurt me no more.* That's when I started making some bad choices. I got mixed up with the wrong kids growing up, but it's like I was still looking. We're all hungry, we're all looking for the reason why we're here and I just took

some wrong, left turns at the right places, ended up where I was and I married when I was seventeen years old. My daughter's dad was the love of my life. I'd like to say he is now, but we went different ways, just doing all the wrong things.

I met my husband when I was thirteen and he was twentyish. He was attractive and I was curious about what was out there. I figured it must be something more than what Mom and Dad were telling me so I went the wrong way. My opening line to him was, "Do you wanna smoke a half joint?" He said, "No, do you wanna smoke a whole one?" I married him when I was seventeen and we rode away together on our Harley. I started messing around with really bad drugs. My friends were the best drug dealers in town and one day, someone said, "You need to go to church." I said, "Really?" I was pregnant and I couldn't stop what I was doing because I was hooked.

The Devil had me. He really had me. My brother in law said, "You need to go to church" and I said, "Why would I want to do that, I'm having fun out here?" He told me "No, you're not having fun because the weekend before, you had a stroke because you over-dosed on cocaine," which I had been using since I was thirteen years old. I had snorted so much coke over the years that my heart didn't want to pound anymore. I had to put my hands and legs above my heart because my heart went nuts. I couldn't breathe and my husband wanted to call the paramedics. I told him, "No, you can't, they're gonna put us in jail or put me in jail."

I started thinking, *I can't do this any more, I want to find a better way.* I was not in the right place and I'm sorry for that because I hurt a lot of people. Years later, God made it all up to me. He showed me the right way and I wasn't hungry for those things I had gone the wrong way with. My parents didn't go to church, but my grandparents, who were our biggest influences and really showed us lots of love, had raised my siblings and me up in the church, but there's that 'Eve thing' that there's something better over here. The kids were saying, "Come over here!" and I did because of peer pressure. When I met my husband, he was wild and crazy too, and we were both looking for something more, it was never enough. When I got pregnant, my friends gave me what I wanted with drugs.

I was six months pregnant when I went to church at my brother in law's suggestion and when I got there, God did a miracle. There's a movie about the end times. It's one of those tribulation movies where they said, "Come forward if you want to know God." I was sitting in church and I heard the voice of God speak to me that day and say, "If you come forward, I will save you and that baby." I was like, "Whoa, I need to go forward." Then I heard the voice of Satan, which I recognized say, "If you go forward, they're all going to laugh at you." I was very aware at that exact moment that there was a spiritual battle going on and I was in it and it was in me.

I went forward and I was feeling the Spirit of God pulling me forward. I looked up and my husband was right there with me and we both fell down at the altar. When we went home that night, I was a different person instantly. I know it doesn't happen instantly for everyone, but it did for me and it had to. I went home and out of habit, I started lining out another line of coke and it was like, *I can't do this, I really can't do this.* My husband said, "Is this gonna help you find God better?"

I had been doing *this* for so long, I didn't know how not to do this. He said, "You don't need this," and I said, "You're right!" He flushed at least one-thousand-dollars' worth of cocaine down the toilet. We could have sold it, but when God changes your life, you become aware that your life is part of everyone else's life in a sense. I followed through and I was baptized and I felt the Holy Spirit guiding me the whole time and I felt my body being completely healed, it was like a miracle.

It's like God took away all the desire to drink or do drugs and I became concerned with being a good mom and that was all that mattered to me. I believed that my baby was affected by my drug use, but God healed her inside of me when I made the choice to give my heart to Him and here I am thirty-four years later and I'm still madly in love with God, but I've had 'falling moments' where I've made very bad decisions, but He was and is still there. I'm the one who walks away. I know that God healed me when I chose Him and the day my daughter was born, there were Angels in that room, I could feel His presence, even the doctor was crying and how many babies did he deliver in his life, you know?

Even though I was in labor for twenty-four hours, we were all caught up in the Angelic presence we felt. I'm not ashamed of my testimony because it's where I was then and I'm not nor, have I been that person since. I feel like we all have a testimony, some people take a work in progress, but God moved mightily and quickly on my behalf. That zeal. Oh my gosh! I remember

that zeal I had for God! Someone said, "It will fade," but it hasn't, thirty-four years later, it hasn't faded.

Years later, after all the bullying from childhood and decisions I made growing up, I would read the scripture, "You didn't choose me but I chose you and I called you out of the world." It made sense and it was healing. The Lord called us and the world can't love us because we're not of this world and that's what I learned, but as a kid, that's probably why I went in directions I wasn't supposed to go because I had to be tough you know and I was good at being tough for a minute. I just got tired of being beat on and kids can be so mean.

Finally, I picked myself up and said, "You're going to hit me? I'm going to hit you first." I once hung out with the Harley guys and that facade was safe to hide behind, but that was never who I was. Now I know that being tender was a blessing, it's not a curse, and I embrace it now. If you want to hurt me, it's okay because I'm not hurt whether you accept me or not. The world's not going to love me, they didn't love Christ, and I'm not of this world.

No one can make you feel inferior without your consent.

-Eleanor Roosevelt

AMAZING TESTIMONY
by:
JESSE CAMPBELL
Instagram: @singjessesing
Facebook: Jessecampbellfanpage
Contestant from the television show
THE VOICE

NOT JUST ANOTHER "PK" (PREACHER'S KID)

I was sixteen and my dad was and still is a Pastor and now a Bishop in Chicago Il. We had a small church on the West side of Chicago. Celebrity gospel artists including The Winans would frequent the church and sometimes stay at our home whenever they came into the city. One day, Ronald and Marvin Winans heard me singing around the house, Marvin told my dad, "Jessie can sing." My dad said, "No, he's a drummer." Marvin repeated, "No, he can sing."

That night, my father gave me a solo to sing at the church. I believe the song was called, "I'll go." I was so nervous you would have thought I was Michael Jackson from the way I was holding myself. My mom politely walked over to me and placed my hand away from my crotch and on my leg. I was surprised that people enjoyed my song and their response made me realize that I could do it, so I kept doing it. I continued singing in the choir for a couple of years and then I formed a group called Gospel Inspirations when I was eighteen or nineteen. David Hollister was also in the group and we performed at various churches, musicals and concerts throughout Chicago.

We all went our separate ways after a few years and three years later I began singing as a solo artist. I went solo because my father would take me on the road with him and have me sing a song before he would speak. We traveled nationwide at least twice a month. Sometimes we would be gone more than that and I didn't graduate from high school on time because of

the road. Dad's focus was church and that's all that mattered and as a result, I graduated my senior year from summer school. I had to sacrifice playing offense and defense as a junior on the football team.

I became a commodity because I could play drums and sing which made the ministry more efficient. I traveled with the organist, Ernie Allen Jr., my first cousin and a trumpet player named Rod McGaha who was 6'7. Rod would stand up from his seat, work his way to the microphone and play his song first, I would get up and sing, and then my dad would preach everyone into a frenzy.

My experience back then is what made me who I am today so I have no regrets. It was just a lot of church. Dad didn't go to football games or graduations. He just went to church. At some point I asked myself, "Why am I doing this? Is it because I want to be in church or I want to be what my dad wants me to be?"

I was blessed to sing and record as a guest vocalist on many different gospel albums, but the business was seldom good and that was not a good experience. It was like everyone would dangle this carrot of righteousness and servitude of Christ before me and I found myself singing on a recording for whatever people wanted or could afford to give me. That just didn't work, with that and how I felt about church overall really brought me to a place of questioning, "Why am I here?"

I came to the conclusion that I am here in church in Christianity because I am trying to be something someone else wants me to be. I was so busy trying to please my father, and the church and what I thought God wanted me to be. When I asked certain questions to my elders, they said, "You don't question God. The word is right by itself and everything will be okay so find your answers in the Word and don't question God."

That was kind of the last straw. I asked questions like, "Who wrote the Bible?" "Why is God only a man?" "What does He look like?" "I don't understand." "Does God need Satan?" "I don't understand!" "How can a camel fit through the eye of a needle?" "What does that have to do with me being rich?" I asked these questions as a kid and I needed answers. They continued to ask me to sing, but I sang from a place of, "I don't understand, but I want to understand," I was confused.

People took that energy during my singing as an anointing, but little did they know the way I truly felt. I didn't like myself and I felt self-pity due to a lack of understanding. The tears

195

would flow while I sang because I didn't even know God, I didn't understand so I was feeling sorry for myself. While traveling with my dad, we went to the Potter's House in Dallas and Bishop T.D. Jakes asked if I would travel with him, it continued.

Even though I had this confusion and I was judging other people who were shouting and dancing all over the church, it was because of the judgment I had of my own self. I didn't know God. I was just trusting that this God is who everyone says He is. I had no testimony, I cried because I saw everyone else crying. I tried to live perfect and every time I fell or made a mistake, I thought I was going to go to hell. I lived and sang in fear. I kept singing for God even though I wanted to do something different. God finally let me know it was okay to ask Him questions and then I began to get the answers. Now I have come to believe that there is nothing to fear. There is no angry God ready to condemn.

I spoke in tongues until my mouth was dry, why would I spend time speaking in unknown tongues? "Shut up Jesse. Speak the words. He can hear a clear thought." These are the things that give me the peace that passes all understanding and that gives me the joy I now know. Coming from a place of fear to now having understanding. How can we get that if we can't question God?

Now it doesn't matter what people think or feel about me, in most cases, they don't even know what they think or feel about themselves. There are so many talented and gifted people in the church that are stuck in the four walls because they are living in fear. I never, ever, have shared this story with anyone, but it needs to be told.

AMAZING TESTIMONY
by:
TIMOTHY TEACH JONES
Actor/Filmmaker/Director/Minister
"DISCOVERING DESTINY"
Social Media: Timothy Teach Jones
(Facebook, Instagram, Twitter)

PURSUIT OF PURPOSE

I came from a two-parent home where I grew up with my five siblings and we had a lot of fun. We would play basketball with each other, "bag" on each other, watch TV together and play cops and robbers. It was the eighties, so we did the normal stuff that kids did back then to stay active and have fun, but we did it together.

Unfortunately, my school experience was different. I dealt with a lot of bullying as a child from my white classmates. I was called the N-word, coon, baboon, porch monkey, tar baby and any derogatory word they could think of to call me daily. The bullying caused me to have low self-esteem.

One day, two white boys who were my age when I was in the second grade jumped me and they beat me up. That incident didn't only hurt me physically, but it also bruised my self-esteem. The boys set the tone for how I was treated and the Caucasian girls followed their lead. I thought the girls didn't like me. If they did like me, I never knew it because they were intimidated by the possible reaction of the boys.

The other traumatic experience I had was witnessing my parents having a conflict at home. They argued and had marital problems when I was around the age of ten and continued arguing all the way through my high school years. I was made to feel like I had to pick a side between my parents and that made me angry. I had to limit my interaction with my dad because my mom was so angry with him for the things he was doing.

197

All of these things prompted me to look for love and acceptance elsewhere. The people who celebrated and liked me happened to be people in the street. It's easy to gravitate to certain activities if the people who are doing them are in your family.

My cousins were gang affiliated and I was seeing them regularly at family functions and although I wasn't raised like that, being around them and being exposed to their lifestyles and their friends influenced me. They loved me, accepted me, laughed at my jokes and it was a good feeling, completely different from what I was experiencing at home or in school.

Hanging out with people in the street drove me to make a lot of bad choices that resulted in a lot of consequences including incarceration. My life was spiraling out of control. I knew what they were doing was wrong from a moral standpoint and from how I was raised, but I knew that the camaraderie my cousins and their friends gave me outranked the risk.

I was with them the first time I drank alcohol. I had a forty-ounce of Old English. I remembered it tasting like rusted pennies. I scrunched up my face because I expected this soda pop flavor, but it wasn't. However, I liked the way it made me feel which made me want it more and more. It made me feel great because it was like medication for all of the pain I was experiencing.

I knew Monday morning was coming and I had to go to school with my knuckles ready. Mom said, "Turn the other cheek and if you don't have anything good to say don't say anything at all," but my thought process was, *if you're dropped off in Baghdad, you better know how to fight.* I became critical and good at bagging on people. I was fifteen, but I felt like a grown man who was in the bar on Friday night and hated having to go to work Monday morning.

I was soon introduced to weed and I loved that as well because it hit my system quicker. The first time I smoked it, I didn't know what I was doing. I thought it was like smoking a cigarette. I watched Ricky Ricardo smoke cigarettes on *I Love Lucy.* He would suck in and blow out the smoke so I tried to copy what I saw him do. My cousin said, "Man, what are you doing? That's not how you smoke weed!" So he taught me how to hold it and breathe it in. It was like a sedative that numbed me. I remember everything in me got relaxed and it made me

feel better than the alcohol did. It made me happy and I laughed at the dumbest stuff in the world.

As a teen, marijuana was therapeutic for me because I laughed the most when I smoked, but then I was back at school and I wasn't laughing during the week. I had to fight during the week, but I was happy on the weekends.

I never graduated to any other drugs, but the alcohol and weed became an addiction by the time I got to college. I knew they were an addiction because I would think about them every day. I couldn't smoke and drink at home around my parents, but when I went away to school and was living in the dorms, I would call my parents and ask them to send me money for books and clothes and spend that money on weed. I drank every day. My confidence was at an all-time high because of the alcohol and weed, but at that time, I didn't realize that it was a false confidence.

Then there were the consequences. One of the first consequences of drinking was when I got a DUI. A lot of people would have thought that would be a wake-up call, but it wasn't because I was addicted. I had two, forty ounces of Old English, Hennessy and gin that day. I had been drinking all day. I didn't feel drunk. My cousins and I got a page from this girl who had a lot of fine friends and we were on our way across town to meet them.

I lost control of the car in front of the police and went to jail that night. I prayed, "God, if you get me out of this situation, I won't drink again." I got in trouble because I was scared. When I got out of jail the next day, I started thinking about the situation and it made me sad, so I had to get medicated again. I drank and got high all that night.

During all of this, I was affiliated with Crip gang members, some of which were killers. Although I never participated in the violent side of gangbanging I loved the sense of family, the brotherhood. These brothers loved me. They didn't make me do anything, they were my friends, but like the Bible says, bad company corrupts good character.

Even though my mom taught me about Godly character, I shielded her from most of my bad choices and the consequences I had to face. She knew a couple of things, but until I did my film about my life recently, she just found out other things that happened in the past.

My communication with my mother was always very general because my parents focused on their marriage issues more than anything. My siblings and I went through a lot and they also had to self-medicate.

The lifestyle I chose drove a deeper wedge between my family and me because I didn't want to be around them when I was high. There were periods when I would go six months to a year without talking to them.

During my darkest moments, I had suicidal thoughts. I remember being in Georgia in college at nineteen, and there was a lot going on in my life. My girlfriend had just broken up with me, my financial aid wasn't approved that semester, I was sleeping on the floor at a friend's apartment, and I walked home from work because I didn't have a car. I couldn't call Mom because we didn't have a good relationship and I couldn't ask Dad for money because that well had run dry.

One day, I was walking home and had planned to jump in front of the next car that passed me, but I didn't have the courage. I waited for the next car so I could jump and I never found the courage to jump with each car that passed. I finally gave up on that plan. The thoughts of taking myself out lasted for the next few years.

I realized at the age of twenty-one that if I kept living the way I was, I was going to end up dead or in jail and that is not where I wanted to end up. In the hood the girls liked me, the guys thought I was cool and I felt like a Hood Celebrity, but no one had the courage to tell me the truth. No one told me I was headed to hell; they all were "Yes, people."

It was a phone call from my brother that saved my life. He basically let me know that God had a purpose for my life and the word purpose seemed like it jumped out of the phone and grabbed me.

It let me know that there was a meaning for me being on this earth, that I had a reason and I had to no longer follow the crowd and do what everyone else was doing, I could actually do me. That led me to discover a lot of my gifts and talents and throw myself into being the best that I could be.

After my brother called and encouraged me, I began this journey searching for my purpose, reading all the books and listening to many preachers. One of the most memorable moments was when I went to Creflo Dollar's church, World Changers International. At the end of his message about life after death, he gave an invitation to the congregation and he said, "Some of you have already accepted Christ, but you haven't been filled with the Holy Spirit and you know there's something missing in your life. Come down now."

Tears welled in my eyes, and I looked over at my girlfriend who was sleeping and my friends who didn't seem interested. I got up and walked down the aisle to join a large group of predominantly black people and was greeted by a young twenty-something-year-old Caucasian minister named Mike who had a long ponytail. He reminded me of a typical California skater you'd see at the beach.

There weren't a lot of white people that went to the church so I was shocked to see this young man and, considering my history with white people, I was immediately disappointed. However, my interest in what God had for me was deeper than the pain and scars from my childhood. Minister Mike lined us all against the wall and he faced all of us. He was very calm and talked to us clearly, "In a moment," he said, "I am going to lay my hands on each of you individually and you are going to feel the power of God."

I was skeptical when I heard this. I watched him lay hands on others and they were crying, but I was determined not to fake a cry. When I was in the street I was real, when I told a dude I had five girlfriends I was honest, when I fought someone, I was authentic. God caught me off-guard. In the Word, it says, "Taste and see that the Lord is good," and the Lord proved to me that day how powerful He was.

I saw Minister Mike approach me from the side of my eye, I was nervous because I knew I was next. When he walked up to me, he laid his hand on my head and began to pray for me. I felt fire come from his hand, the Holy Spirit came into my body; I felt like I was electrocuted and I was shaking all over. I felt like God hugged and embraced me. I cried for the rest of that day.

I walked out of the church to my girlfriend and her friends and when she saw me crying she said, "Awe boo, it's going to be okay, let's go get some lunch," but she really didn't understand that my life had changed. I cried all the way to the restaurant and all the way home. I knew that day I would never be the same again and not too long after that, my girlfriend and I broke up.

God grabbed me. Once you've had a close encounter with God himself like the woman who fought her way through the crowd to touch the hem of Jesus' garment and was healed by her faith, you will always sense His presence. It doesn't mean that I am sin-free, but I am grateful. He is my life long companion and through his daily mercies and my daily repentance that gives me confidence. The ironic part is, God used a white man to bring me closer to Him.

After that day at World Changers International, I never went back to smoking marijuana and never became a drunk again. God has blessed me with two beautiful daughters, and by the grace of God I'm determined to be a godly example for them.

I set out to inspire other people, especially young people, and I encourage them not to make the same choices that I did as a kid so they wouldn't suffer those same consequences. I wrote, produced, and directed my life story in a riveting documentary entitled *Discovering Destiny*. The tagline is; One man's pursuit of purpose.

I found out what the key to happiness is and that it is serving other people. So, I will live a satisfying life knowing that every gift that I have is supposed to be used to empower, to educate, to inspire and to entertain people and I guess that's why they call me, "TEACH."

Break through your brokenness. Step out of your hopelessness and discover that you're an overcomer!

-Trisha Mann-Grant

SCRIPTURES ON
OVERCOMING SETBACKS

---

¹ The Lord is my light and my salvation — whom shall I fear? The Lord is the stronghold of my life — of whom shall I be afraid?
Psalms 27:1

¹³ For I am the Lord your God who takes hold of your right hand and says to you, Do not fear; I will help you...
Isaiah 41:13

⁹ Do not be quickly provoked in your spirit, for anger resides in the lap of fools.
Ecclesiastes 7:9

³ Not only so, but we[a] also glory in our sufferings, because we know that suffering produces perseverance; ⁴ perseverance, character; and character, hope. ⁵ And hope does not put us to shame, because God's love has been poured out into our hearts through the Holy Spirit, who has been given to us.
Romans 5:3-5

⁵ Trust in the Lord with all your heart and lean not on your own understanding; ⁶ in all your ways acknowledge him, and he will make your paths straight.
Proverbs 3:5-6

²⁸ And we know that in all things God works for the good of those who love him, who have been called according to his purpose.
Romans 8:28

⁸ We are hard pressed on every side, but not crushed; perplexed, but not in despair; ⁹ persecuted, but not abandoned; struck down, but not destroyed.
2 Corinthians 4:8-9

203

2 Consider it pure joy, my brothers and sisters,[a] whenever you face trials of many kinds, 3 because you know that the testing of your faith produces perseverance. 4 Let perseverance finish its work so that you may be mature and complete, not lacking anything.
James 1:2-4

God is so much better at running our lives than we are,

if we just commit to Him.

CELEBRITY CORNER ENCORE TESTIMONY

Throughout this book I have testimonies by people of all walks of life. Each person in this book is just as important as the next and some of them are even celebrities, including my own husband, Tony Grant, who has two testimonies in *Amazing Testimonies*. I chose a very special lady, however, to feature on this Celebrity Corner page.

I have had the pleasure of working with this dynamic woman on stage productions by Priest Tyaire called *Mrs. Independent and Momma's Boy* who took the time to share her heartfelt testimony with us. Shirley Murdock has been successful in the R&B world of music as well as the gospel arena. Her heart is just as beautiful and golden as her voice. I don't have a chapter that deals with the pain of mourning a loved one, but Mrs. Shirley tells a true story of how she dealt with the death of her mother, father, and manager.

Many people have lost themselves after the loss of a loved one. Depression, hopelessness and thoughts of suicide try to overtake those who are mourning, but Shirley Murdock offers some pearls of wisdom that help us to remember that we can do all things through Christ who strengthens us and God's grace can get us through such a terrible storm.

AMAZING TESTIMONY
by:
SHIRLEY MURDOCK
Singer
Twitter: @ShirleyMurdock Instagram:
@ShirleyMurdock4Real
Ministry: Praying4You.org
www.ShirleyMurdockLifeSongs.com

TEARS OF SORROW TO JOY

October 29, 1998 was the worst day of my life. It was the day I lost my mother.

When I got the devastating news, I looked up to Heaven and said, "Lord I know you won't put more on me than I can bear, so if I'm here, I must be able to bear it, not because I'm so strong, but because of who you are and with you I can do all and bear all." I knew that the only chance I had at surviving this was to call upon everything I heard, read, and experienced about the Lord and it had to kick in and kick in *now!*

My heart was broken and there wasn't a day that went by that I didn't miss my mother. Weeks later, while on my knees, crying and grieving, the Holy Spirit spoke to me and said, *"That wasn't about YOU. That was about HIM keeping HIS promise to HER, that after her work was done, He would take her home to rest!"*

Then I said, "Mama, how can I deny you the promises of God?
You *made* it! I'm *happier* for *you* than I am sad for *myself!"*

That was the moment my bitter tears of sorrow turned to sweet tears of *joy!* The joy of knowing that to be absent from the body is to be present with the Lord. The joy of knowing that whatever we've lost, God has found, and that He never leaves us empty. He gives us beauty for ashes, the oil of joy for mourning, and the garment of praise for the spirit of heaviness. Don't get me wrong, I still cry sometimes, because I miss her, but a smile comes to my face because I know where she is and I know that one day I'll see her again and *never* have to say goodbye!

We know that it's not until the olive is broken that the oil is released, and I have discovered that God makes us stronger in the broken places. I understand that I have oil anointing healing for those broken where I have been broken.

The devastating loss of my mother prepared me for the tragic loss of my manager and producer six months later, followed by my dear father. So when I find myself facing difficult situations that require me to *walk by faith and not by sight*, I remember that the Lord is the same yesterday, today and forevermore.

He was able to sustain me during what I declared to be the worst time of my life, giving me confidence in the fact that if He could do it *then*, He can certainly do it again and again.

Now I draw from my past experiences, to fuel my faith, so that I no longer walk by regular faith, but by hi-octane!

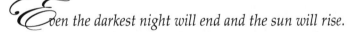

Even the darkest night will end and the sun will rise.

Victor Hugo

When we do the best we can, we never know what miracle is wrought in our life, or in the life of another.

Helen Keller

About The Author

Trisha Mann-Grant is an Award-winning actress, writer, and motivational speaker born on the south side of Chicago, Illinois. She started acting and singing in grammar school and in her senior year of high school she began doing print work for *Ebony* and *Jet* magazines, posing for Raveen Hair, Fashion Fair Cosmetics and other products for a ten-year span. In 1990, Trisha won the title of MISS BLACK CHICAGO and used her crown to speak to and motivate students across the city. Trisha also became a member of Delta Sigma Theta Sorority, Inc. of Lambda Chapter.

Seven years later, Trisha relocated to Los Angeles, California and diligently pursued her acting career. She began doing many stage plays, toured the country with David E. Talbert's, *His Woman His Wife*, starred in short films that eventually led to feature films and she also booked co-starring roles on many sitcoms, including Tyler Perry's, *LOVE THY NEIGHBOR* opposite her husband Tony Grant and the series *Cold Case*. She tours with Andre Pitre and Charnele Brown's Theatrical Musical, *CHANGES*. She had more musical stage tours and her latest nationally, theatrically released film, *The Man In 3B*, can be seen on NETFLIX, BET and on DVD.

Trisha's experiences in the entertainment business as well as "life" experiences inspired her to write, produce, and direct various projects as well. She is the creator of MANN TALK, a talk show focused on the views of men of all walks of life who gather to discuss relationships, divorce, marriage, politics, sports and more. Her dearest project to date was her God-given stage play, *Mama's Will* that Trisha wrote, directed, and produced and will soon release as a book along with *A Single Mother's Blues*. The journey of the production *Mama's Will* is a testimony all of its own. Trisha is grateful to share her experiences and those of others under the guidance of the Holy Spirit.

In addition, Trisha is the U.S. Ambassador and Director on the board of BOOKER AUTISM FOUNDATION OF LEARNING (Bafol). She also sits on the board of HELP ME HELP YOU organization for the homeless.

With all the triumphs, Trisha has experienced many heartaches and tribulations as well. She overcame being bullied at different schools while growing up, escaped an abusive relationship, lost a major record deal, survived a stroke, struggled through two unexpected pregnancies, experienced being homeless and refused a doctor's negative report about her unborn child then declined his invitation to have a legal abortion. These are just a few of the chapters through Trisha's life's journey that have made her have a heart for others who are hurting or are oppressed. When asked if she would do it all over again she said, "I wouldn't change a thing because each experience taught me and brought me to be the woman whom God has made me to be.

"I am a walking AMAZING TESTIMONY."

Trisha presently resides in California with her husband, Tony, and two children, Dena and Daniel.

Feel free to follow Trisha at:

INSTAGRAM-TRISHAMANNGRANT621
INSTAGRAM-amazingtestimoniesthebook
TWITTER - @TRISHAMANN
IMDB - TRISHA MANN
FACEBOOK – Trisha L. Mann-Grant
FACEBOOK – Trisha Mann-Grant
FACEBOOK – Amazing Testimonies with Trisha Mann-Grant
www.trishabooks.com
www.trishamanngrant.com

If you have a true testimony or you know someone that does, please let Trisha know that you are interested in sharing your story at trishabooksnow@yahoo.com

Made in the USA
San Bernardino, CA
12 November 2018